Hold Nothing Back

Hold Nothing Back

Writings by Dorothy Day

Edited by
Patrick Jordan

Foreword by
Kate Hennessy

LITURGICAL PRESS
Collegeville, Minnesota

www.litpress.org

Cover design by Monica Bokinskie.

This publication is an abridged and updated edition of *Dorothy Day: Writings from* Commonweal, ed. Patrick Jordan (Collegeville, MN: Liturgical Press, 2002).

1   2   3   4   5   6   7   8   9

Library of Congress Cataloging-in-Publication Data

Day, Dorothy, 1897–1980.
    [Essays. Selections]
    Hold nothing back : writings by Dorothy Day / edited by Patrick Jordan ; foreword by Catherine Hennessy.
        pages   cm
    ISBN 978-0-8146-4655-7 — ISBN 978-0-8146-4680-9 (ebook)
    I. Jordan, Patrick, editor.   II. Commonweal.   III. Title.

BX4668.D3A5   2016
242—dc23   2015033945

*In grateful memory
of three Catholic Worker exemplars:
Frank Donovan,
Ed Forand,
and Kassie Temple*

Peter Maurin always says that it is the duty of the journalist to make history as well as record it.

—Dorothy Day
Commonweal, November 3, 1939

Contents

Foreword

Dorothy Day was a prolific writer. This is a miracle in itself given the tasks she faced as cofounder—or "housekeeper" as she called herself—of the Catholic Worker and as mother and grandmother to both her own family and to all she gathered about her. Dorothy's relationship with *Commonweal* magazine spanned from when she was in her early thirties and the single parent of a young girl to when, at the age of seventy-five, she was a grandmother, venerable leader, and potential saint. Already a successful journalist and novelist, her first *Commonweal* article was published four years before the beginning of the Catholic Worker Movement and her life in the public eye. *Commonweal* also played a crucial and serendipitous role in the formation of the Catholic Worker when its managing editor at the time, George Shuster, sent to Dorothy a French peasant with ideas for Catholic social justice. His name was Peter Maurin, and within months of their meeting Dorothy and Peter launched the *Catholic Worker* newspaper. During the early years of the movement, *Commonweal* was known to donate money at dire times, in addition to sending eminent scholars to speak at the Worker's Friday night meetings. The circle of this relationship was completed, in a sense, when one of the Catholic Worker's own, Patrick Jordan, became *Commonweal*'s managing editor.

The articles in this volume are a small representation of what Dorothy has written, but they contain glimpses of much of what inspired and compelled her. The writings that provide the greatest poignancy for me are those in which she describes her daughter (my mother) Tamar Teresa. These have allowed me to know more about my own mother and the deeply connected relationship that she and Dorothy maintained throughout their lives. Six articles center on Tamar (whom Dorothy refers to as Teresa). "Guadalupe" is an account of a pilgrimage as experienced by a four-year-old Tamar. "Bed" is a tale any parent would recognize of putting a child to bed. Nighttime discussions with my mother could run to the theological and philosophical, as well as issues of wealth and poverty. "Now We Are Home Again" contains one of my favorite quotes from my mother: "Flowers and grass and things are so beautiful they just hurt my feelings." This one sentence provides a delightful intimation of the woman Tamar would come to be. I also recognize Dorothy's habit of singing "All Ye Works of the Lord" to Tamar, which continued and grew in length as each of Tamar's nine children were born.

In these early years, Dorothy provides a sense of what would, as I see it, come to be one of her greatest strengths as a writer— her weaving of the personal and familiar with both her interior life and explorations of a wider, deeper nature. What seems simple description in her writing often contains much of what lies beyond. An intimate portrait of Tamar also touches on the mysteriousness that a young child can contain. Visits to gardens not only include the names of flowers but elicit the names of Maxim Gorky and Charles Dickens. Within a portrayal of life on Staten Island, Dorothy writes of a reoccurring sense she experienced—beginning when she was a child and that would continue to her last years—of both the immensity of God and "glimpses of hell" without God.

There are many other aspects of my grandmother's writing that I find nourishing and are represented in this collection. Her loving obituaries and portraits describe people my mother knew well. Her vivid and evocative sense of place—whether Mexico,

Staten Island, the Mott Street Catholic Worker house, or her New York City neighborhood—helps me to see elements of the sacred that may be found anywhere one looks. Her stories are sprinkled with sketches of friends and strangers of all backgrounds, of those in need of help, and of those for whom it is too late, and I am left feeling they were all members of her family—and what a mighty family it was! These are jewels of thought and observation, and they feel like blessings coming from her sharp-yet-loving eye.

This volume also provides glimpses into how the Catholic Worker movement unfolded. Two months before the *Catholic Worker*'s first issue was published, Dorothy writes of helping a newly poor family search for an apartment. As the Depression deepened, her writing begins to focus on the lives of the unemployed and underemployed. She witnesses these lives with detail and clarity, and then she imagines what could be with so little, beginning with willingness and commitment. From this we are brought into the early years of the Catholic Worker soup line and house of hospitality. In 1938, five years after her initial meeting with Peter Maurin, there appears within Dorothy's writings a deeper sense of maturity, and the phrases "works of mercy" and "voluntary poverty" drive much of her thoughts. She provides lessons on how to start a house of hospitality and warns of the danger of believing that if one can't do it right, one shouldn't do it at all. (She often quoted the phrase, "The best is the enemy of the good.") The essential tasks for Dorothy were to give it one's all and to have faith during those interminable tasks of cooking and cleaning while rarely having enough food or beds to go around. She also reminds us of the holy intimacy of sitting down to eat together.

Dorothy often concludes her instructions with a plea for help. She reveals something of the time she spent traveling around the country speaking publicly and appealing for funds, food, and volunteers. Only her daughter and those closest to her knew just how agonizing these talks were for her and how difficult it was for Tamar and Dorothy to be apart.

This collection is also, of course, a portrait of Dorothy's faith. The saints, whose company was vital to how she kept her strength and faith, were present in her thoughts from early on. A meditation on the Blessed Mother includes a discussion of the beginnings of her Catholicism as influenced by two communists and how, before her conversion, she learned to say the Rosary by reading a book. Dorothy also returns often to the theme of being on pilgrimage, and, like she did for so many things, she held a wide and embracing concept of what a pilgrimage could be—whether it was a bus ride through the Midwest, life at the Catholic Worker, or a visit to Our Lady of Guadelupe in Mexico.

By 1949, her voice displays a heroic sense of strength, vision, and power. Dorothy is now asking the hard questions. How far can one live in voluntary poverty while remaining able to do what needs to be done? How can one be Catholic in the face of the church's wealth and the luxury in which so many clerics live? What does it mean to go to jail, and why should one do it? And perhaps the most difficult of all—how does one continue the work despite an unrelenting sense of failure?

This series of snapshots covering a large portion of Dorothy's life concludes when, at the age of seventy-five, she is stripped of so much—her health, energy, and youthful enthusiasm—to reveal a profound state of gratitude. Dorothy Day has given us many gifts, and the gift I find among the most sustaining is how she compels me, in the most gentle of ways, to strengthen my sense of *gratitude*. I am not aware of which grandchild it was who wrote on Dorothy's birthday card "because you are very, very old." It could have been me, as the youngest grandchild, although I have no recollection of it. It would be gratifying to feel so included in this collection of her writings, but nonetheless I am truly grateful to witness, through these *Commonweal* articles, Dorothy's passage from the young mother of a single child to the spiritual grandmother of such a multitude.

Kate Hennessy

Preface

Dorothy Day (1897–1980) is considered one of the most interesting and prophetic American Catholics of the twentieth century, a fact alluded to by Pope Francis in his September 24, 2015, address to the US Congress. Born in Brooklyn to a non-churchgoing family of journalists, she combined a rugged, personal quest for authenticity with a lifetime of practical idealism. A convert to Catholicism at the age of thirty, she immediately cultivated a deep appreciation for Scripture, the life of prayer and the spirit, and the sacramental riches of the church. As an American Catholic laywoman, she wed her distinct writing craft, sense of history, and love of literature to serve the common good and to reform society.

In 1933, Dorothy Day and Peter Maurin (1877–1949) launched the Catholic Worker Movement. Its aim was to bring the social implications of the gospel "to the man in the street" by living with the poor, practicing the works of mercy on a daily basis, and resisting war and participation in industrial society's never-ending preparations for war. This distinctly lay undertaking ran counter to the thrust of much of American society and the church's own self-preoccupations; it anticipated many of the emphases that would later emerge from the Second Vatican

Council (1962–1965). In fact, Dorothy Day was in Rome twice during the council. At its final session, she fasted and prayed for a strong condemnation of nuclear war and modern warfare's indiscriminate slaughter of innocent noncombatants. The council strongly endorsed these points in its 1965 Pastoral Constitution on the Church in the Modern World, *Gaudium et Spes* (see especially chapter 5 of that document). Dorothy Day went to jail repeatedly to protest war and to call for just and nonviolent social change.

Perhaps one of Dorothy Day's most telling personal traits, however, was her approachability. There was in her an unmistakable appreciation of others—a sense of enjoyment of them and of her own immediate family. She conveyed a sense of gratitude toward others that had the effect of making one feel welcome and valued. Her daily bread and sustenance, throughout a grueling life shared with the poor, was her practice of what Peter Maurin called "the primacy of the spiritual." It is hoped that this short book, gleaned from some of her writings for *Commonweal* magazine from between 1930 and 1973, will not only introduce readers to her writing but also to the rich spiritual foundations that were the basis of all she wrote and did. Dorothy Day's insight and spiritual wisdom only deepened with her years, nourished as they were by her daily spiritual reading, participation at Mass, prayers, sacrifices, and sufferings.

Unlike some writers on the spiritual life, Dorothy Day was neither a professional theologian nor a trained confessor. What is unique and inspiring in her writing is a candid, lay perspective on the daily and historical situations that she examines and addresses. She repeatedly draws herself and her readers back to the heart of the gospels: to their challenge and the grace they provide for assessing life's immediate situations. She writes about life as a pilgrimage, one that for her included: raising a small child as a single parent; leading a disparate, challenging lay movement; and traveling to the far corners of the country and beyond, often on crowded buses, in order to cover breaking stories and write about them. Then there are her struggles to pay the bills and to keep up with her growing family, all the while continuing to protest the exploitation of workers and minorities and to witness for peace. Clearly, one of her lasting legacies is that she wrote in such a way as to inspire and encourage her readers. Like the poor widow in Luke 21:1-4, she held nothing back. We must go and do likewise. Dorothy Day can help us learn how: one day—each day—at a time.

Patrick Jordan

Guadalupe

1

"Today," I announced to four-year-old Teresa, "we will go out to see Our Lady of Guadalupe."

"A pil'mage?" Teresa asked hopefully. Pilgrimages to her whether in New York, California or Mexico, mean very delightful bus rides, and in general a spirit of festivity. "I will bring Mary flowers." She always speaks of our Blessed Mother in a most familiar way. And forthwith, she began to strip heliotrope blooms from the plant which blooms in my French doorway, looking out over the roofs of Mexico City.

I put a stop to this depredation, telling her that we would buy flowers from a little boy in the market, but she stubbornly clung to a few, too short-stemmed blossoms.

Teresa is at a very precious age, the age when the apocryphal stories tell us that Saint Anne introduced the Blessed Virgin to the temple. The little girl Mary danced up the steps, the story says, and I remember it often when Teresa is inclined to be full of antics in church.

Originally published in *Commonweal* 11 (February 26, 1930): 477–78.

Busses are always crowded, but more exciting than street cars. We got in at the Zocalo, in front of the cathedral, and within a few blocks, two sheep got in too, or rather were pushed in, for their feet were tied together, and they lay on the floor of the bus at our feet, surveying us patiently. In front of the driver's seat hung a picture of Saint Christopher, and beneath the picture a little vase suspended for flowers. We were reassured by the presence of the Saint, for the bus careened madly around corners, past other busses, narrowly escaping pedestrians, urged on by the shouts of the conductor at every corner, "*Vamonos*," and by a vigorous slap of his hand on the tin sides of the camion.

The conductor is a gentleman beneath his rags. He gets out of the bus to help old ladies on. He lifts off the babies and children. He holds the market baskets for the women going home from their shopping. At one time, he had three gayly bedecked baskets, full of flowers, tomatoes, squash, one with a rabbit and still another with a live chicken, and in spite of his armful, he managed to collect the fares and help people on and off.

Teresa's enthusiasm was infectious. She squealed loudly at the spectacle of the lambs, the chicken and the rabbit. She wanted to know why there wasn't a pig.

"I'll sing a little song—all about a little pig riding on a burro, and all the little pigs have dirty faces—and that is Mexico."

No one could understand her song but the passengers laughed with her and the man next to us said, "*Muy contento*," and asked us where we were going.

Though the busses race along at a delirious speed, they are not impolitely hasty. If the driver sees anyone a block away indicating by gestures that he would like to come aboard, he stops to wait, and takes out a little top, which spins in the air, a "jo-jo" it is called, and which all the men and children are playing with at this time in Mexico City. But not the women. They have no time to play. They go to market and to Mass. They are always washing clothes. When they have nothing else to do, they are fanning the charcoal fires in order that the men and the children may eat.

Guadalupe is only a few miles from the center of the city, not as far as the Bronx is from lower Broadway. It takes only twenty minutes to get there. Though Christmas and Epiphany are passed, it is always a holiday at this shrine of the patroness of Mexico. December 12 is Guadalupe Day but the pilgrimages are not confined to the holiday season. Throughout the year tens of thousands of devout natives with their padres, come from distant cities in special trains to worship at their Virgin's shrine. As our Lady of Lourdes revealed herself to the poor peasant girl, so did our Lady again reveal herself to the poor peasant Juan Diego, filling his tilma with roses that he might convince the bishop— it was so long ago that it was the first bishop of Mexico—that his story of her appearance was indeed true. When he dropped the roses out at the feet of the bishop, his tilma was imprinted with a glorious picture of the Virgin, which is just as bright and glowing to this day as all the bright prints and reproductions which hang in every home, in every shop and market and place of business.

In front of the cathedral where the picture is enshrined are many booths where rosaries, candles and pictures are sold. On one side is a huge covered market which spills out into the streets for blocks around. On the other side there is a park where a Ferris wheel and merry-go-round accompany with their clamorous music the prayers of the faithful in the church. And in the back, there is the hill of Tepeyac where the Aztecs lived before the Spanish conquest. Now the hill is surmounted by a cemetery and on the top is a lovely little chapel which looks out over the entire city of Mexico, surrounded by the mountains, of which the greatest are the Mujer Blanca and Popocatapetl, crowned with dazzling snow. Nestling close to this small church are many little adobe houses, built on the side of the hill.

After Teresa had blessed herself with holy water, and made her rather lopsided genuflection, she skipped out of the church again that she might lean over the low walls and peer into doorways at the chickens, pigs, lambs and pigeons, not to speak of cats and dogs which shared the houses and gardens.

"These are all Mary's babies," she said. "The little pigs and the chickens and the boys and the girls. And these are all little baby houses, and that," pointing to the church, "is the mama house."

It had been a hard climb up the slippery cobbled steps of the little hill, and we were glad to sit there for a while on one of the terraces looking down on the pueblo of Guadalupe. On a pilgrimage the devout Mexicans will climb that hill on their knees, but on ordinary days like this they content themselves with a lesser penance. When they enter the cathedral at the foot of the hill, they advance on their knees all the length of the church to the altar, holding aloft a lighted candle in their hands. Many mothers have bundles on their backs as well as babies in their arms as they humbly pay their respects to the Mother of God.

When we descended the steps on the other side of the hill, there was still the holy spring to visit which is sheltered by a chapel domed with glazed tile. The spring boils up in the bottom of the walled-in well, and Teresa leaned over it fascinated. Attendants brought up water in copper buckets and poured out jugs full for the Mexicans and Indians who surround it at all times of the day, in order that they may drink.

"And oh, the tiniest baby church!" Teresa shouted, looking across the street where the littlest and humblest of chapels has been erected in honor of Juan Diego. There is room for only eight or ten people in it and it is the width of its doors which always stand open. Teresa had to say one of her tiny prayers here, "about you and me," she explained, and then she was ready for the bus again.

"And now, no more churches today," she sighed, surfeited as even the great saint for whom she was named confessed her weak flesh at times to be—"but a lollypop and peanuts instead."

Bed

2

Teresa, four and a handful, sat at the library table with her crayons and paper in front of her and tried to ignore the fact that it was getting dark outside and that it was time for her to go to bed.

I sat at my desk trying to write letters.

"Here is a picture of a man, a man dancing and telling a whole lot of stories. He's playing on his catarrh too, and singing songs. Are you listening?"

"That's a lovely picture, darling," absent-mindedly.

"And here is a little boy, and he stays out in the garden all day, not in the house any more, because people are naughty to him. *Lookit!*"

"Uh-huh."

"*Lookit!*"

"Yes, I see, sweetheart."

"And this is just a man, *muy feo, muy feo. Muy grande boca, muy grande* ears, *asi*, and tomorrow I'll make three of four ears on him. Isn't he a terrible man? *Are you looking?*"

Originally published in *Commonweal* 14 (May 27, 1931): 100–101.

Teresa's conversation as well as her pictures were influenced by her recent stay in Mexico.

"And this is a kitchen with all the dishes hanging on the walls, and here is the Holy Ghost and there's fire-crackers in the kitchen and a fiesta. It's so much noise, I must go outside and play with the childuns. And the Virgin Mary is out there too with a little tiny baby, and this is a picture of me dancing, and the Virgin Mary is dancing too and there are leaves all around. *Do you hear me?*"

The clock struck eight.

"I don't wanna go to bed! I don't wanna go to bed!"

"But you have to go to bed, so come on, honey, and I'll help you unfasten."

"I can do it myself. Lemme do it myself!"

Then one of those hectic half-hours which mothers know. The bath; the shower, insisted upon to top it off; the splashing all over the bathroom floor; the desire, combated, to mop it up; the giving of the eight drops of concentrated cod liver oil, treated by violet ray, guaranteed to put on eight pounds a week, an elixir of life (only maybe it is the orange juice in which it is given which does the trick); the nightly battle over whether to wear "jamas" or a "nightie"; the insistence on the box of chessmen under the bed to wake up on in the morning.

Then prayers, repeated after me, begun in a kneeling posture, continued in a sitting, relapsing finally into some sort of gymnastic posture.

"*Teresa!*"

"What!" in pained surprise.

"Either sit down or kneel down, but for goodness' sake keep still."

"Won't the Virgin Mary like it if I try to stand on my head?"

Unanswerable question. I'm sure she does like it, but what is one to say?

"Now come on, hurry up and finish."

"I don't want to hurry up," piously. Teresa continued with a long list of people and things to be blessed by God, and then with a virtuous sense of duty done, she hopped into bed.

"What about a kiss?" she asked coyly.

"Here is a kiss." But it was too definite a one.

"I want lots of them."

"Mm-m. Lots."

"I want tickle kishes. Tickly kishes in the neck."

"There now, that's enough," very firmly.

"But I wanna drink o' water."

"Here."

"Lookit. A little moss in the glass of water." The little moth which had flown in from the garden just to complicate matters, was dumped down the wash-bowl.

"Did you throw it away?" "Yes."

"Is it dead?" "Uhuh."

"Did it get drowned?"

"Probably, and now for goodness' sake go to sleep."

"But I can't. I can't stop laughing. I'm laughing because Ernest was an elephunt. Isn't it funny that Ernest was an elephunt? I'm going to laugh and laugh until I have hiccups. Then you'll have to bring me another glass of water. All night long, you'll have to bring me a glass of water."

I have held Milne's poem of Mary Jane and her "rice pudding for supper again" against him, and now I was beginning to resent his famous elephant which was causing all the giggles.

The small voice rambled on. From the sitting-room I could hear it as it was intended I should.

"Doddee! Are you listening? I want to tell you a story. Once there was a little mouse and a bunny rabbit and the bunny had jamas on and a pretty little hat and he went to the mouse's house for supper and they had bumana and puddum for supper."

The story went on. The requests for attention went on.

"Are you listening to me? Why don't you answer me? I'm not going to sleep. Do you hear that I'm not going to sleep? Why didn't you tell me the story of Old Mother Cupboard who lived in a shoe and had so many childuns she didn't know what to do with them all? And what did Humpty Dumpty fall off the wall for? Was he a naughty boy and did his mama tell him not to climb up? You didn't cut out any paper dolls for me tonight. You didn't let me color the paper dolls that you didn't cut out. You didn't let me—"

There was no end to the things I had not let Teresa do that evening and which she wanted to do besides sleep.

"I want my doll in bed with me. Do you hear me?"

Feeling somewhat guilty by my child's recriminations, I got up and fetched her favorite doll.

"I'm going to tell my doll on you. You wouldn't let me—"

The small accusing voice continued. . . . And then—suddenly I realized that I had been reading for five or ten minutes in complete silence. Once more the nightly miracle had been accomplished. Teresa had fallen asleep.

Now We Are Home Again   3

For two long summers I have been away from my little house on the shore of the island. We had rented it to friends and had gone traveling and working elsewhere. Now we are home again, Teresa and I, to find the garden overgrown with weeds, my perennials strangely distributed around the neighborhood and no longer in my own flower beds, fish-lines and ten-foot poles strung around the room, a box of dead and dried worms and clams left under a couch on the back porch, and fish-hooks stored on the little shelf over the door where a cross used to be and where now a giant spider crab hangs on the wall.

The crucifix had been moved and hung in the attic, which Teresa and I make our sleeping quarters, and in the bustle of spring cleaning and homecoming I did not transfer it to its usual place for some weeks. In those weeks the rain poured down, the wind howled dismally around the house, I sprained my knee digging clams, Teresa had another attack of malaria, I was tormented with poison ivy, three short stories were turned down by magazines and in general life was dismal.

Originally published in *Commonweal* 14 (August 19, 1931): 382–83.

One evening as Teresa was getting ready for bed and knelt to say her prayers, she turned around to the shelf over which the ugly, but biologically interesting, specimen hung.

"There is no cross there," she said, "so I'll just say my prayers to the spider crab."

Then and there we delayed the going to bed until the shelf had been nicely dusted, a little rose-studded shawl from Mexico hung over it, and the crucifix brought down from the attic and a few hyacinths from the garden placed in front of it.

We both slept very well that night, in spite of the howling of the wind which sounded like devils battering against the little house. I can laugh at myself for my Irish forebodings, but I believe in devils as I do in angels. I have heard them before in the gloomy melancholy of the wind and have felt that I have had a glimpse of hell in a sudden knowledge of the horror of the absence of God. I have felt a devil in the shape of a little fly which buzzed about my ear as I walked two miles home on a hot summer afternoon, after I had been gossiping with a friend about a neighbor.

But now with the spider crab hanging from a nail over the dining-room table in its proper place, the sun has come out, Teresa is better, my poison ivy is gone, my young brother has his first job on the country paper, I have been given work for the summer in the way of garden interviews, and life is serene and happy once more.

The island is ten miles long and four miles wide and, although there is a railroad running from one end of it to another, it would be necessary to walk miles and miles to interview the members of the horticultural clubs. So though my salary did not warrant it, I have bought myself a car. It is eight years old and it cost only $35.00. But with license plates, new tires, and the things that needed adjusting such as the carburetor, coils, wires, etc., I found that within a couple of weeks I had paid $75.00, all told. Now it is running smoothly and Teresa and I whirl around the country roads at a dizzying speed (twenty miles an hour) and stop off at old farmhouses and beautiful estates and dingy, little new houses and bright and shining new houses, and talk to their occupants about flowers.

We find people raising other things too: alligators, large ones, in little greenhouses; bull frogs in fish pools; newts and salamanders in terrariums; turtles, birds, rabbits, even snakes. Teresa thinks my job is great fun, especially since she is often presented with flowers and plants for her own little garden, and other things, such as a parasol, and a kitten!

She had long wanted a kitten but we had been traveling around so much that it was impossible to keep one. It is true we had two little ones in Xochimilco, Mexico. We got them when we were living in our stone house with the thatched roof, to scare away the field mice which ran across the bed at night. The kittens didn't do much good. We locked them in at night, but in the morning they used to run back to the Indian's wattle hut next door where there was a fat pig and several turkeys, both alive and in the shape of *mole* plentifully spiced with peppers, to keep them company, inside and out.

But our kitten here is very much with us. He thinks his tray of sand is to play in, and he jumps in and out, scattering sand all around, hunting for an occasional pebble. When I cuffed him the other day for a misdemeanor—very cold-bloodedly, for I was in a happy humor and only meant to remind him that some things aren't done—Teresa looked at me with astonishment.

"You made my eyes get swampy when you did that to my little cat," she said reproachfully.

It is fun to get in the car and go jouncing along to see new places and people, and both the places and people are very nice, having to do with flowers and birds and beasts as they do. We jump and leap occasionally, "like a goat" Teresa says, but generally the car runs smoothly. Once we got stuck on the side of Grymes Hill, where Maxim Gorki and Dickens visited when they were here. (Little is known about their stay.) It is a very steep hill, and I bore down on the foot brake so hard that my sprained knee started hurting grievously.

"We just can't do anything," Teresa said in her resigned way, "so we'll just admire the scenery." We were concentrating on this when a truck came along and nosed us up to the top very kindly.

We never telephone people we are coming, because the nicest ones are the quiet ones who don't like to be interviewed, and we find that it serves better just to walk in on them and trust to luck that they will be hospitable and talkative about their plants. Mrs. Stirn, a nice old German woman, was a pleasant refuge to us after our strain and excitement of getting there, and we sat on her terrace looking out over the Narrows, and talked of Capri and Axel Munthe and many other things besides flowers, while Teresa tried to catch a little snake which had clumsily fallen down out of the rock garden into a tiny pool of water which was made there for birds and rabbits.

Our own garden is not doing so very well. The soil is full of clay which hardens like cement; the five pounds of grass seed which I sowed have been blown away or eaten by the starlings, and what is left is coming up in a most haphazard manner. But the irises which used to form a hedge around the house and are now in clumps, are bursting into flower, and the forsythia is blooming like bursts of sunshine around the house. Just beyond my little lawn and the wild cherry and apple trees, the ground dips sharply to the sands, which are as yellow and as warm as ever. The bay is a calm gray blue today, and the little waves chuckle along the beach.

Every afternoon we lie in the sun there and keep very still to hear the last of the gulls who are on their way further north for the summer and to listen to the water and the land birds. Sometimes Lefty, who has a vocation for poverty, comes out of his shack, where he lives winter and summer, and skins eels and washes clams for his supper and keeps us company. He does not like money, nor need it, and lives by exchange, bringing a mess of fish to the barber for a haircut and digging worms for fishermen in exchange for groceries and loaning out his boat for kerosene to fill his lamp. He heats and cooks in his little shack by a driftwood fire.

Down in Mexico I had the endless lagoons of Xochimilco on every side, with the mountains rising up around them. Here are the long reaches of the bay. Down there I was surrounded by a garden full of violets, roses, cactus flowers, calla lilies and pomegranate trees, but never a blade of grass. Here is green, lush green, everywhere.

Down there in the country I lived in a house where the doors and windows were of solid oak and had to be taken down in the morning to let light into the place. It is a land which cannot afford glass windows in the country places. But here there are six windows looking out on the meadows, the sands and the bay.

I am very glad to be home again, to be cultivating my own bit of soil, to be living in my own house and to feel, for the time at least, that I am never going to leave it again. There is beauty here too, a lovely, gentle beauty of cultivated gardens and woodlands and shore. We picked flowers the other day in the woods—dogwood, wild lily of the valley, quince blossoms, blueberry blossoms and the last of the violets. Along the road we gathered sweet clover to put in the hot attic, where its fragrance will be distilled and fill the house, and Teresa sighed happily, "Flowers and grass and things are so beautiful, they just hurt my feelings."

East Twelfth Street 4

When we came back to New York from our visit to Florida, Teresa and I, we had an opportunity to rent our little summer place for six months, so we were faced with the necessity of finding a home for ourselves and furniture to put in it. Hotel bills being exhorbitant, we were in a rush, and in a few days we found a comfortable tenement apartment, with steam heat, hot water and plenty of sunlight—all for $28.00 a month, in the warmly crowded neighborhood of Avenue A and Twelfth Street. It was early spring with a cold tang in the air, very refreshing after the torpid heat of Florida. We had both sunlight and warmth, and best of all, a huge expanse of sky to look out upon, owing to the presence of a long low garage on the other side of the street. Every night we could watch the sky in the south change from rose to violet, and as the spring advanced, there were the early storms to enjoy, massive clouds, pierced by lances of lightning, sheets of silver rain against the purple dusk. It is a luxury indeed to have acres of sky to look out upon in New York City.

Originally published in *Commonweal* 17 (November 30, 1932): 128–29.

"We have the two most important things right on our street," said Teresa, thinking of the miles we had to go in Florida to reach a church. "You can go to Mass every day and leave me home to play, and I can go to school and leave you home to work. I don't need to go to church, do I, because we have plenty of praying in school? Too much sometimes."

The school, which was one she had attended before, is a day nursery just down the street, run by the Helpers of the Sacred Heart. Babies of one year old and up are taken care of, children of the first three grades are taught, and the children who have passed on to higher grades and are attending other schools, public and parochial, in the neighborhood, come back to the nursery for their luncheon and for after-school activities. There are 275 children taken care of all day long by the Sisters, in addition to the children who come in for meals. The place is large and roomy, and there is a roof garden and a backyard and a play-room under the roof for recreation.

One of the Sisters of the order heads a Sunday School too, which takes care of 1,200 young ones in the district who attend public school.

"Today," said Teresa, "I had four dishes of spaghetti. It was very good."

"It must have been."

"There was one little boy who had six. But he was a *cochina*. He is always hungry. Every afternoon after school when we have bread and jam or bread and cheese—if it's bread and cheese, I give him the cheese."

Lunch is not confined to spaghetti alone. Perhaps there is pineapple or stewed apricots for dessert. And bread and milk too.

The nursery is open from seven in the morning until six at night, and children are cared for all day and fed practically two meals a day for $1.20 a week.

At this time, where there is great talk about provision made for the babies and little children by the Soviet government, it is good to call attention to the fact that Mother Church has always kept in mind the pre-school child. There are nurseries in every section of the city for the child of the working mother. The state and city, except for clinics, have always ignored the needs of the child under kindergarten age, and those attending kindergarten are only cared for three hours a day. What other nurseries there are, are either very expensive affairs, charging from $30.00 to $75.00 a month, or else works of charity, run by brisk social workers for the "lower classes."

Little Teresa attended one of these her first and second winters, and I shall never forget the painted chairs on which the little ones sat and sat, and the painted toys (to be looked at) on the shelves, and the uniforms covering the heterogeneous garments of the poor, and the briskness, the terrible briskness, of those in charge. I remember coming early to the nursery one winter afternoon, in time to get a glimpse of child after child being propelled with horrid speed in and out of the washroom, and the worn and haggard faces of the attendant looking forward to the end of the day. Thank God, the Sisters think in terms of eternity. There is never that unpleasant hurry.

The church across the street from us is an Italian church, and there are dramatic funerals very often, with a band accompanying the hearse down the street to the church. The automobiles move along at a funereal pace, the band, when it is not playing, drags its many feet with a shushing along the asphalt, and as the cortege approaches, the bell from the church tower tolls a single spaced note, a dread and mournful sound. The music is triumphant and soul-stirring, lending an especial poignance to the spectacle.

To Teresa, this glimpse of death with its massed flowers, its dignity and solemnity, has lent a new aspect to heaven. A year ago she had said, "I do not want to die and go to heaven. I want to stay where there is plenty of fresh air." And this evident impression of a stuffy heaven which she had in some way or other visualized, dismayed me. She was thinking of the grave, I assured her, and not of a heaven which was filled with not only all the present delights of her life, but many more.

"Beaches?" she wanted to know. "And many little crabs and snails and pretty shells? I do want to live on a beach in heaven." And I assured her that there were indeed beaches in heaven.

The brass band and flowers of the Italian funerals lent emphasis in some way to my recital of heavenly joys and she said contentedly that if either of us got there first, we would wait for the other.

Along the side walls of the church are glass-enclosed statues: Our Lady of the City, Our Lady of Perpetual Help, Our Lady of Grace, Our Lady of Mt. Carmel, Our Lady, Help of Christians and Our Lady of Lourdes. In addition to the usual statues of Saint Joseph, Saint Anthony, Saint Thérèse and Saint Anne, there are those of Cosmos and Damien, Saint Sebastian, a fine figure of Saint John the Baptist dressed in real sheepskin, and Blessed Don Bosco in a little shrine all his own.

There was a tremendous procession which stretched for ten blocks around the church on the feast day of Our Lady, Help of Christians, and though the day was cold, there was a line of white-clad girls wreathed and garlanded and carrying banners. It was impressive to see the older women, bent and twisted by life, holding aloft the banners of their faith, on which were emblazoned the insignia of the associations and confraternities to which they belonged. . . .

As I mentioned before, there was not only the problem of finding a home, but furniture to fill it, since all my belongings were in the country. I was able to bring in two beds, my sister contributed chairs and a table, other contributions were forthcoming in the shape of wicker furniture, pillows, rugs, etc., and my younger brother, whom we sometimes call Brother Juniper, insisted upon making me some furniture. His bookcases looked solid until books were put into them, and then they teetered dangerously. His benches could not be sat on. The table he constructed for my typewriter looked so heavy and solid that I was deceived into a feeling of security about it and began using it at once.

It is my custom when possible to attend Benediction. ("I am perficky able to mind the house and take care of myself," Teresa says.) So one evening, on coming in at eight thirty, I was startled to hear shrieks and wails of neighbors coming from my front room. I sped up the stairs, with my heart pounding, and found Brother Juniper's table in pieces on the floor, and my typewriter and papers in wild confusion all around. Teresa and Anita, the little girl next door, had merely bumped into it and the table had gone down.

My neighbor with Jewish emotionalism had rushed to the rescue and, seeing that it was my means of livelihood which had fallen on the floor, and fearing that her child had had some part in the desecration of my desk, she had started her wailings which had brought the whole house to my door.

Little Anita was Teresa's constant playmate after school all through the spring. Not old enough to go to school herself, she insisted on coming in to play school, or "Make for fun you're my baby and I'm your mama," was one of the games. Anita is very tiny, with long hair which hangs in pigtails on either side of her fat face. She and Teresa were very fond of each other, and it was hard to drag them apart at bedtime.

"Let me stay just until she gets into bed," Anita said. "Let her stay just until I say my prayers," Teresa added.

And this custom of letting Anita stay made Teresa forget that sometimes there were too many prayers and that some of them were too long. I myself did not know how many prayers she knew until she used them all as a means of letting Anita stay, and then I heard, for the first time, the Creed, the Acts of Contrition, of Charity and of Hope, in addition to the Lord's Prayer and the Hail Mary. When the bless-thems came along, Anita waited with breathless interest until her name too was mentioned among the friends and relatives.

It was Anita who started the game of "Make for fun we are two ladies with lots of little babies and we must go to visit the Lady Mary." So they sat with their doll carriages beneath the statue on the mantelpiece and talked of tonsilectomies and feedings, while the figure of Our Lady of Grace, which has been blessed by a Pope and has traveled from Rome to Spain, to South America, to New York, presided with a benign smile over two little girls of East Twelfth Street.

For the Truly Poor 5

Maria has come in from the country where she has been living for the past years, and we are going out to look for an apartment for her. It is for herself, her two children and husband. Without money they could no longer get along in the country. The city offers Alan a job at $15.00 a week and now the problem is, finding a home. The family of four cannot live on $15.00 a week, you say? Nonsense! With courage and determination, one can do anything. Well, of course, if they are used to it. . . . But they are not. They are used to owning their own home, to having a car, to sending their children to a private school.

But Maria meets problems with a fine spirit and refuses to be defeated.

It is one of those keen, clear January days with a faint warmth in the air—a good day for a brisk walk. Starting south on Avenue A, we face a sharp wind and a dazzling winter sun which hangs low over the houses. It is early, only two o'clock in the afternoon, and it is amazing how much light and sparkle there is in that sun which hangs so low in the sky.

Originally published in *Commonweal* 17 (March 15, 1933): 544–45.

We have no set plan, Maria and I, that is to say, we do not really know where we are going to look. We are just setting out to walk up one street and down another until a likely place presents itself. Nevertheless, I more or less know what I am doing, for I have placed the whole matter in the hands of Saint Joseph. He is a fine one to find a home for you, I tell Maria.

Maria is a Communist, but she is very fond of me, and if I think Saint Joseph is going to guide us, well and good.

He should be especially helpful, I add, since he had so much trouble himself in finding a place for Mary and the Child, and in consideration of the fact that we are modest in our demands, not expecting much more than a stable for the rent we can pay, he will surely guide us.

On 15th Street, just across from the Immaculate Conception Church, there is an empty flat. But though the outside of the building is clean, the inside is not, and the rent is exorbitant. Twenty dollars for four rooms, no heat, no hot water, no bath! Impossible. We are not being finicky, we just know we can do better.

As I say, we had no plan on setting out, but we did intend to confine our researches to one area—that large sprawling part of the East Side, bounded by the Williamsburg Bridge on the south, 14th Street on the north, the East River and Avenue A. This is a section apart from subways and elevated trains and accessible only by meandering buses or crosstown cars, which means that to get anywhere you have to pay two fares. But Maria likes to walk and so does Alan, and he can get up a half an hour earlier to make the long crosstown hike and save carfare, and the walking will be enlivening and he won't miss the country so much.

We are finding the walk enlivening ourselves, and as we go, we peer through doorways, looking for backyard houses.

Did you know that all over the East Side there are hidden streets, accessible only through front buildings or obscure alleys, and on these hidden streets there are sometimes stables or little houses or rows of apartment buildings hidden from the world? These are quiet places, away from the noise of the street, away from trucks and taxis and street cars, and often, if the houses in front are high and those in back low, away from sunlight and air too. But sometimes the position is reversed, the houses in back are high and those in front low, and there is apt to be a bargain there.

One such place we found, back of Avenue A. It was a tall, slim backyard house, four stories high, an apartment to a story, and each apartment renting for $14.00 a month.

But the janitor's husband reeled at us dangerously, and the smell of alcohol sent us fleeing to the street.

We cut over through Tompkins Square, to get to Avenue B, and it was good to feel the spongy earth under foot, though the feel of it brought a nostalgia for the fields.

Down on 8th Street past Avenue C there was an old house (not a backyard house) facing north and south, with a trampled back yard. But the rooms were large and light and high-ceilinged, the house was a well-built one, and despite the neighborhood, which was teeming with children, one felt the luxury of space and nobly proportioned rooms. There were well-appointed bathrooms, good electric fixtures, a well-outfitted kitchen. But the rent for this place was too high, $25.00, and the gas bill would bring it up to $35.00, what with the heating of both house and water; and a man getting $15.00 a week cannot afford that, said Maria firmly.

Cutting across Avenue C which is a wide sunny street, we passed the pushcarts piled with artichokes, tomatoes, mushrooms and all kinds of fruits.

"A penny a piece for artichokes," I cried, buying some, "and mushrooms only fifteen a pound. One can always eat anyway."

. . . We cut back along 7th Street toward the part where the school children are beginning to gather for play. This street is not as crowded as 11th, 12th or 13th. Those are supposed to be rough streets. Seventh Street has synagogues and women sitting out in the sun with baby carriages. On one side there is a public school. Around the corner on the square is St. Bridget's Church, with a parochial school in back.

We were nearing the corner when we passed a wide passageway leading back to a long irregular-shaped yard where there are a half-dozen five-story buildings. In front, facing the street, the houses are only three stories high.

The son of the Russian janitor, a clean, spectacled student, opens the door to one of the houses and shows us the apartments. There are three rooms, of fair size, all of them light and sunny on the top two floors. The living room has a fireplace and two many-paned windows facing south. The bedroom and kitchen face north and there is a window in each. There is a little toilet off the kitchen. Instead of a washtub, the boy says, the landlord will put in a bathtub. There is no heat, no hot water, no electricity, but the rent is only $10.00 a month.

The houses are sordid, grim, and look as though they belong in a Dickens novel. But Maria, who believes in scrubbing with strong yellow soap, is thinking of blue and white check curtains at the windows and her blue rag rugs on the floor.

"Blue, the psychologists say, is a happy color," she says cheerfully, not at all taken aback by the seven years' accumulation of dirt in the apartments, for it is long since they were occupied, the janitor's boy says.

"Blue is the color of the sky and the Blessed Virgin's robes."

"If we take the top floor, we can use the roof. There'll be plenty of blue then. Alan can build a fence to make it safe for the children."

Her mind is pretty well made up—Saint Joseph has helped us in our search, for really, the rooms envisaged with fresh paint, curtains, scrubbed floors, rag rugs and children's toys, are not so bad. A clear eye and a courageous spirit has transformed them into a home.

But it is too fine a day not to continue our walk, so we venture further into the depths of the East Side, down to Stanton Street to visit the model tenements of the Lavanburg Foundation. . . . Here there are roof gardens and basement club rooms, a kindergarten, and community activities. But the rents are $30.00 for three rooms . . . too much for working people these days, when fathers of families are working half or full time for $10.00 and $15.00 a week and glad even of that to hold body and soul together.

"What should be done," said Maria, "is this. Landlords with the cooperativeness or sense of duty or whatever you want to call it, of Mr. Lavanburg, should take their old houses where the poor are still forced to live because they can't pay more than $10.00, $15.00 or $18.00 a month, and utilize the basements and roofs. There could be mothers' and fathers' clubs, and children's play clubs to meet in basement rooms for their activities. Community spirit and cooperation would be fostered. And the roofs could be made into playgrounds where they could gather together in summer instead of on crowded front stoops and garbage-filled streets, where the children are in continual danger. It wouldn't take much to make these reforms: only a landlord who has a social conscience and a few tenants who would cooperate and get things started. You don't have to have a million to do it. You don't have to have steam-heat and hot water. The poor are used to hardship. Small beginnings," she ruminated, as we walked back through dusky lamp-lit streets, for it was now five o'clock and twilight was upon us. "The roof playground first. . . . We'll see what we can do. . . ."

Saint John of the Cross 6

"We are poor, but we are also rich," said Teresa sagely, in reference to a remark of the little girl upstairs whose mother had just bought a new kitchen stove. "As long as we have a roof over our heads and a few spoonfuls of food, we are rich."

"But I want more than a few spoonfuls of food," said Dickie, who was having dinner with us that night and who has a healthy twelve-year-old appetite. "I want two or three helpings."

So dishing out some more baked potatoes and string beans, I began to regale them with the poverty of Saint John of the Cross, whose life, by Father Bruno, I had been reading for the past week.

I told them about the hermitage of Calvario where Saint John lived for a time. The former prior there had been unbridled in his ascetism. The only food he allowed his hermits was raw herbs selected by Brother Alonso the cook, who led his mule along the mountainsides and looked at what it fed on so that he might collect it.

Originally published in *Commonweal* 18 (July 14, 1933): 287–88.

"A good many of them would have preferred that he should cease from troubling himself," the account written at the time reads.

On feast days they had a stew of breadcrumbs seasoned with oil, garlic and pepper, and so strict were the hermits that some criticized this relaxation as unnecessary.

"I would have eaten the mule," said Dickie stoutly buttering himself another slice of bread. "They ate horses during the war. I guess I coulda eaten mules."

"But Saint John wasn't so strict," I hastened to assure my guest. "He said that 'as men's minds are more inclined to society than to solitude, it was necessary in hermitages one should have a little more well-regulated corporeal solace than elsewhere,' so he must have remedied the scanty meals at Calvario, and then it could not have been so bad."

According to the account of Father Bruno who traveled all over Spain in the footsteps of Saint John, Calvario was a beautiful spot surrounded by orange, fig, almond and olive trees. The trouble with the place was that it was so small that the brothers were crowded and could not be alone. So at night John used to take them walking and after recreation by the banks of the stream which ran past the hermitage, he scattered his hermits to various points on the mountainside to make their evening meditation in peace and quiet.

"That is like us," said Teresa, spooning up her apple sauce. "Down in the country we have such a little, little house, it is like the colored people's houses down in Florida. So when we want to get away from people, we go walking on the beach and sing 'All ye works of the Lord.'" "We never have enough room anywhere," said Dickie, who is a big fellow and finds it hard to dispose of his arms and legs. "If the rooms aren't too small, then there are always grandmothers and relatives hanging around and telling you to turn off the radio."

Saint Teresa, the good friend of Saint John, loved poverty dearly too. "The great honor of the poor is in being really poor," she says in her "Camino." But she adds that she made Saint Joseph her banker and never hesitated at any useful expenditure. "She was too supernatural and too intelligent to do things by halves," Father Bruno says. She herself writes, "Saint Teresa and three ducats is nothing, but God, Saint Teresa and three ducats is everything."

One of her first aims in her new houses was to see that her nuns had enough to eat, though she herself had to skimp often. One of the evils of the unreformed order lay in the fact that the convents were so poor (Reverend Father Rubeo after visiting them in 1567 forbade them to receive any more novices "for they would be in danger of dying of hunger") that the nuns fell into lax habits of sociability in order that they might receive from the hands of their friends sweetmeats and dainties to eat.

Saint Teresa not only loved poverty but she had a great respect for poor people, just as Saint John of the Cross had, and she was too "supernatural-minded" to turn away Andrada, the ragged young student at Toledo who offered to help the Sisters. "He had nothing but himself to help them with, he said," Saint Teresa writes in her "Foundations." "It amused me much and my companions more, to see what sort of assistance the holy man (Brother Martin of the Cross) had sent us; for his appearance was not that of a person for barefoot nuns to associate with."

But she asked him to find a house for them, which he did in a day. He told them it would be cleared out and for them to bring their things, and he expressed no surprise at the two mattresses and one blanket which Saint Teresa and her two companions had. "We went for some days with the mattresses and the blanket without more to cover us, and one day we had not even a bit of wood to broil a sardine," she writes. "At night we suffered a little from cold, for it was cold; however we covered ourselves with the blanket and with the serge cloaks which we wear over our habit, which have often been useful to us."

"She can't have been much more uncomfortable than I was all last winter," said Teresa's uncle, who is six feet and also young and gangling, "on that bed which folded up and had ridges in the middle and a mattress two inches thick. But I slept all right," he added.

I commended his saintly patience and continued my talk of the saints of those days. There were a great many of them—not only Saint Teresa and Saint John of the Cross. Father Bruno tells of Anne of Jesus, Beatrice of St. Michel, Catherine of St. Albert, Magdalene of the Holy Ghost, Frances of the Mother of God, Catherine of Jesus, Anne of Lobera and Marie de la Cruz. Catherine of the Conception, the holy Portuguese, was so gay "that she went to heaven laughing," as Saint Teresa put it.

They were all very gay and happy as a matter of fact. Blessed Anne of St. Bartholomew who knew Saint Teresa better than anyone, tells us "that she did not like melancholy people, that she herself was not gloomy and did not wish others to be so in her company; she used to say, 'May God deliver me from surly saints.'"

When Saint Teresa entered her convent to take the habit as a young girl, she went there dressed in an orange-colored dress with black velvet trimmings. She was always lighthearted—and I picked up Father Bruno's book to read some of it aloud.

"Teresa, like Saint Peter of Alcantara," he writes, "did not insist so much on mortifications of the flesh as on *desnudez*, the solitude and silence so necessary and fruitful for the spiritual life. . . . The primitive rule does not prescribe absolute silence, save from after Compline to Prime of the following day. Teresa, in order to put a stop to unnecessary conversation, settled on two hours of recreation, one in midday, the other in the evening, during which time 'things are so combined that we learn to know our own faults, at the same time enjoying relaxation which helps us the better to support the austerity of the rule. But the slightest detraction is strictly forbidden.' There is nothing cold or formal about these recreations she speaks of, which are so useful for acquiring self-knowledge. They have not the slightest appearance of prescribed duties. The Sisters chat as they work, for Teresa did not intend them to be idle. This does not prevent gaiety, even though there was no great desire for laughter. . . .

"In her, the mystical impulse, poetry and childlike gaiety were all in harmony. She said to some peevish Sisters who took scandal, 'All this is needed to make life endurable.' Father John was not scandalized, and he acted in the same way more than once. He is a poet, the poet of the dark night, but also the poet of joy and love."

Before reading Father Bruno's book, I was acquainted with Saint John of the Cross only through the writings of Saint Teresa and through some translations of his poems. I knew very little about him, and though I was sure he was not a surly saint, I had thought him an extremely solitary one. So I was glad to find in Father Bruno's pages that his brother, Francisco de Yepes, was always his very dear friend and followed him in his wanderings often. And Catalina Alvarez, his mother, who had been left a widow early to support her two young sons by her silk weaving, came to his house at Duruelo from her home in Medina in order that she might cook for the Fathers in the first house of the reformed Carmelites. I thought as I read of the devoted Catalina, how Don Bosco's mother sold all that she had in order to help her son in his work for the youth of the city streets, and how she too came to live in his first house to help with the cooking and cleaning.

He was indeed poor, but, as little Teresa says, "he was also rich," this valiant saint!

Houses of Hospitality 7

In the Middle Ages when one out of every four was leprous, there were two thousand leper houses run by religious in France alone. This is the startling and thought-provoking statement made in Farrow's book, "Damien, the Leper." That statement has not been contested. It may be horrifying to make such a comparison, but inasmuch as one out of every five workers today is unemployed or on work relief, the catastrophe which has visited us is comparable.

Unemployment is the gravest problem in the country today. It is immediate, so it is more pressing than the problem of war and peace. It means hunger and cold and sickness right now, so it is more immediate a problem than the unionizing of workers. In fact the unionizing of workers cannot get on while thirteen million men are unemployed and those employed are hanging on to their jobs like grim death and not willing to make any forward steps which would jeopardize those jobs. And we contend that the kind of shelter afforded these unattached unemployed is liable to make them leprous in soul and utterly incapable of working for sustenance or salvation.

Originally published in *Commonweal* 27 (April 15, 1938): 683–84.

There are thousands of men sheltered in the lodging houses of New York City, run by the city, and countless other thousands sitting up all night in missions and flop houses and roaming the streets. As the weather gets warmer you may see them sleeping in the shelter of buildings, in areaways, in subways, along the waterfront. They crawl into their holes by night, and by day come out to tramp from one end of the island to the other in search of food. Every other city—Pittsburgh, Boston, Detroit, Chicago, Milwaukee, St. Louis—has the same problem.

Peter Maurin, whose idea it was to start the Catholic Worker, began it with a simple program which called for round-table discussions, houses of hospitality and farming communes. Before the depression, he predicted it. During the depression he constantly stressed the problem of unemployment. He is still journeying from one end of the country to the other, speaking of a new social order wherein man is human to man and which can be built up on the foundation of the works of mercy and voluntary poverty.

He himself has been a transient worker and an unemployed worker. He spent twenty years traveling through the United States and Canada, doing the manual labor which built this country. And it is due to his constant indoctrinating, as he calls it, that groups in New York, Boston, Pittsburgh, Chicago, Detroit, Milwaukee, Troy, St. Louis, Houma, Louisiana, and Windsor, Ontario, have started what Peter himself called from the beginning houses of hospitality, where those in need can receive food, clothing and shelter, and hold round table discussions, which point to the solution of problems. Peter is only doing what the great Saint Peter called for—working for a new heaven and a new earth, wherein justice dwelleth.

In New York, the unemployed come from all over, seeking work. They are not all single men. There are the married, as well as the sons of the family who leave home in order that they may not be a burden on those that remain. There are whole families migrating. There are young married couples. There are even lone women and girls.

Peter has always pointed out that according to canon law, all bishops should be running hospices, or houses of hospitality. But now, thinking in terms of state responsibility rather than personal responsibility, those in need are turned over to agencies, to the city or the state. There are isolated instances of hospices of the homeless of course. I have visited Father Dempsey's huge hospice in St. Louis, for instance. Father Dempsey was criticized for "bringing all the bums in the United States to St. Louis." But nevertheless his work was well supported and he was able to carry on his work for many, many years. There is a splendid hospice run by the St. Vincent de Paul Society in San Francisco, where a small charge of $.15 is made. There is a day shelter besides where men can remain during inclement weather. We believe of course that an absolutely free place is necessary for the wanderer not having any funds or not knowing the ropes. I have heard of a hospice in Philadelphia which I wish to visit, and doubtless there are many more. I hope readers of this article will let me know of others throughout the country, run under Catholic auspices.

I have visited all the hospices run by Catholic Worker groups, naturally, and they all have the same difficulties and the same problems and are all run on the same lines. They all started with no funds at all. A small group got together, decided they wanted a headquarters for propaganda and meetings, and rented a store for $10 or $15 a month. None of them ever knew where the next month's rent was coming from. Usually there was no money for paint or soap or mops or beds or stoves or cups. But little by little these things were contributed. Most of them began fearfully and are continuing fearfully. If any of them ever thought they were going to have to feed the numbers they are feeding, they would never have had the courage to start. (Oh, we of little faith!) Most of them hesitated along for several years before starting the endless task of feeding those who came. For as soon as the feeding began—as soon as the mood of hospitality began to make itself felt—lines formed at the door, and continued day after day.

In New York, our breakfast line, which began with a single friendly pot of coffee on the stove in the store where we hold our meetings, grew and grew until now we serve breakfast to approximately 1,000 men. They begin forming on the line at four-thirty in the morning. The door is not opened until six and then the work goes on until nine or nine-thirty. During the day we have only sixty or so to the other two meals. We have to consider the work of the paper, letter writing, receiving visitors, taking care of those under our roof which number about fifty in the city and fifteen in the country. (In the summer there will be about fifty there too.)

In Boston they feed 250 men a day; in Pittsburgh 200; in Detroit, 400; St. Louis, 200; and so on. The numbers are not so large, but if the reader will just contemplate saying to himself, "Two or three friends and I will undertake to feed 350 people a meal every day," not just for one day but indefinitely, stretching out month after month, year after year, he would be aghast. Just try it. He would not think it possible by himself of course, nor would he trust the Lord to fall in with his seemingly presumptuous plans.

Yet if we are thinking in terms of personal responsibility, to those who sit around and say, "Why don't the priests do this or that?" or "Why don't *they* [that indefinite *they*] do this or that?" we should reply, "Why don't *we all*?"

It is really the work of the lay apostolate. In this day of huge parishes, running into thousands of souls (sometimes even 10,000) it is hard to see how the priest can think of undertaking such a work. Bishops used to have personal knowledge and acquaintance with not only all their priests but many of their flock, whereas now the bishop of a large diocese has every moment taken with spiritual duties.

We not only believe that this is the work of the lay apostolate, but we believe that all over the country the faithful should gird up their loins, so to speak, and start two thousand houses. If France could start and continue for a few generations two thousand leper houses, until segregation, combined with the plague, wiped out leprosy, then surely we in the United States ought to be able to open and continue two thousand houses of hospitality and face the prospect of continuing them not only through this generation but until the social order has been reconstructed.

It is a grave emergency. The Holy Father says that the workers of the world are being lost to the Church. If we are all lay apostles and "other Christs" this is our responsibility.

Trade union leaders like John L. Lewis believe that through strong unions, labor leaders in politics, legislation, the thirty-hour week, insurance, taxation, and public works financed through taxation of industrialists rather than of the poor through sales taxes, the unemployed can be reabsorbed and those not reabsorbed can be taken care of.

Perhaps a Christian state could do all these things. But since we are living under only a nominally Christian state, Christians will have to resort to those old-as-the-Church itself methods of the works of mercy through houses of hospitality to care for immediate needs such as food, clothing and shelter.

These needs supplied under Christian auspices would make a startling change in the character of the unemployed. Hope, that most sinned-against of virtues would be restored. Hospices in the shadow of churches would mean a constant recognition of Christ the Worker, Christ our Brother. . . .

As it is now, under the dubious hospitality of the city and state, it is as though God were unknown. There is no reminder to morning and evening prayer. Men have lost the sense of their own dignity, that dignity which they possess because Christ shared their humanity, their unemployment, their dire need.

The House on Mott Street 8

In view of the fact that all workers in the New York house of hospitality live on Mott Street instead of in scattered homes as they do in our other centers where there are only one or two in charge, it may seem that there are many to do the work in New York. But our staff is not so large [and] Peter Maurin and I are traveling and speaking a great deal. . . .

New York has more than its share of visitors so we have many guests who are interested in the work and in the social ideas of Peter Maurin. Often we have visitors from early morning until late at night, coming to every meal and remaining for discussions which go on at all times of the day, when two or three are gathered together. (I recall one such discussion when last summer three young priests met for the first time at the Catholic Worker— one from California, one from Texas and one from New York— and have been fast friends ever since. They spent the entire afternoon with us and stayed to supper.)

Because of the crowds of callers and visitors for one or two weeks' stay, it is harder to get all the work done sometimes than

Originally published in *Commonweal* 28 (May 6, 1938): 37–39.

if we had just two or three running the place. More people means more work, as every woman knows. The fewer there are, the less there is to do. The fewer there are running one particular work, the more gets done very often. Witness a clumsy committee of thirty as compared to a committee of three.

Other groups contemplating starting a house of hospitality will argue, "You have the paper to help support the work." Yet experience has shown that the work gets support wherever it is started, and the support continues. Some fear that they will withdraw local support from the New York group and the paper. And yet, in spite of flourishing houses in the big cities of Boston, Pittsburgh, Detroit, Chicago, Milwaukee and St. Louis, they keep going and so do we.

It is true that it is never easy. God seems to wish us to remain poor and in debt and never knowing where we are going to get the money to pay our grocery bills or provide the next meal. While writing this, we have nothing in the bank and are sending out an appeal for help this month.

But we are convinced that this is how the work should go. We are literally sharing the poverty of those we help. They know we have nothing, so they do not expect much and they even try to help. Some of our best workers have been recruited from the unemployed line. They are not going to a magnificent building to get meager aid. They are not going to contemplate with bitterness the expensive buildings to be kept up, and perhaps paid for on the installment plan, and compare it with their state. They are not going to conjecture as to the property and holdings of the Church and criticize how their benefactors live while they suffer destitution.

The trouble is, in America, Catholics are all trying to keep up with the other fellow, to show, as Peter Maurin puts it, "I am just as good as you are," when what they should say is, "I am just as bad as you are."

There are no hospices because people want to put up buildings which resemble the million-dollar Y.M.C.A.s. If they can't do it right they won't do it at all. There is the Italian proverb, "The best is the enemy of the good." Don Bosco had a good companion who was always not wanting to do things because they could not be done right. But he went right ahead and took care of his boys in one abandoned building after another, being evicted, threatened with an insane asylum and generally looked upon as a fool. Rose Hawthorne who founded the cancer hospital at Hawthorne, New York, started in a small apartment in an east side tenement, not waiting for large funds to help her in the work.

Once the work of starting houses of hospitality is begun, support comes. The Little Flower has shown us her tremendous lesson of "the little way." We need that lesson especially in America where we want to do things in a big way or not at all.

A small store is sufficient to start the work. One pot of soup or a pot of coffee and some bread is sufficient to make a beginning. You can feed the immediate ones who come and God will send what is needed to continue the work. He has done so over and over again in history. We often think of the widow's cruse when we contemplate our coffee pots. When the seamen during the 1936–1937 strike asked us where we got the wherewithal to feed the fifteen hundred of them a day who wandered in for three months, we reminded them of the loaves and fishes. And they had faith in our goodwill, and in our poverty too, for many of them took up collections on their ships after the strike was over to try to repay us. We have four seamen still with us, two of them joining the movement with their whole hearts and contributing everything they have to it. One came back from a trip and gave us all he had, $160.

What is really necessary, of course, and it is not easy, is that one put everything he has into the work. It is not easy to contemplate, of course, but for those who feel called to do the work, if they honestly give everything they have, God takes care of the work abundantly. We have to remember the case of Ananias who was trying to hold out, even while he wished to enjoy the privileges of belonging to the group. . . .

"The little way," faith in God and the realization that it is He that performs the work, and lastly, not being afraid of dirt and failure, and criticism. These are the things which must be stressed in holding up the technique of works of mercy as a means of regaining the workers to Christ.

We have read so many advertisements about germs and cleanliness and we think so much of modern improvements, plumbing, prophylaxis, sterilization, that we need to read again, thinking in terms of ourselves, what our Lord said to His Apostles: "Not what goeth into a man, but what proceedeth from a man defileth him."

Please understand that we are not averse to the progress of science. We think of cleanliness with longing and never hope to achieve it. We spend money on food instead of on fresh paint and I defy anyone to make an old tenement clean with plain scrubbing. Antique plumbing, which goes with poverty and tenements, cold water, no baths, worn wood full of splinters that get under the nails, stained and chipped baseboards, tin ceilings, all these things, besides the multitudes that come in and out every day, make for a place that gets pretty dirty. And we get plenty of criticism for it, the justice and injustice of which must be acknowledged. Sometimes it rains or snows and then two thousand feet tracking in the muck from the street makes the place hopeless. But if we waited until we had a clean place before we started to feed and house people, we'd be waiting a long time and many would go hungry.

Peter has always stressed the value of manual labor, and that the worker should be a scholar and the scholar a worker. He also firmly believes that those who are considered leaders must be servants. Christ washed the feet of His disciples.

So in the history of the Catholic Worker, we have all done a good deal of cooking, dishwashing, scrubbing of toilets and halls, cleaning of beds, washing of clothes, and in a few cases even of washing human beings. (Once Peter and I were scrubbing the office over on 15th Street, he starting at the front and I in the back. And Peter, believing as he does in discussion, paused again and again to squat on his haunches while he discoursed, I having to stop in order to hear him. It took us all day! He is a better

scrubber than he is a dishwasher. You have to put all your attention on greasy dishes when you heat all the water to wash up
after sixty people. Another time I was washing baby clothes for
one of the girls in the house of hospitality and Peter joined in
the rinsing of them. Now there are so many of us on Mott Street
that there is a distribution of toil, and a worker is liable to take
offense if his job is taken away from him even for a day, regard-
ing it as a tacit form of criticism. But on the farm there is always
plenty of opportunity for the most menial tasks.)

Also, most important of all, one must not be surprised at
criticism. We all find it hard to take, and one good thing about
it is that it shows us constantly how much pride and self-love
we have. But take it we must, and not allow ourselves to be
discouraged by it. It is never going to be easy to take, and it is a
lifetime job to still the motions of wrath on hearing it. Criticisms
such as these:

"What good does it all do anyway? You don't do anything
but feed them. They need to be rehabilitated. You might better
take fewer responsibilities and do them well. You have no right
to run into debt. . . ."

In regard to the debt, all of us at the Catholic Worker consider
ourselves responsible for the debts we contract. If our friends
did not come to our assistance, if we did not make enough by
writing and speaking and by publishing the paper to pay them,
and if therefore we were forced to go "out of business" as the
saying is, we would all get jobs as dishwashers or houseworkers
if necessary and pay off our debts to the last farthing. And our
creditors know this and trust us. At that, we have fewer debts
than most papers, considering the coffee line and the number of
people we are supporting.

All criticisms are not reasonable. One woman writes in to tell
us we must get separate drinking cups for all the men. A man
writes to tell us to serve oatmeal and a drink made of roasted
grains and no bread. For a thousand people! And the latest criticism is the following, written on a penny postal and not signed.
It is the second of its kind during the week.

"Out of curiosity I stopped at your bread line today. I saw several men making (as they term it) the line two or three times, actually eating the bread in the line. This is the schedule of a number of the men in whom you are interested: 1st trip, South Ferry, breakfast; 2nd trip, morning, 115 Mott Street; 3rd trip, morning, St. Francis, West 31st Street. I heard Jack tell Tom he must go right then to Water Street, be there not later than 11:45 so as to be in time for South Ferry at one o'clock." The writer ventures to say that "95 percent of your men are not worth powder to shoot them."

God help these poor men, traveling from place to place, wandering the streets, in search of food. Bread and coffee here, bread and oatmeal there, a sandwich some place else, and a plate of stew around noon. Never a meal. Many of them lame and halt and unable to travel, and living on a sandwich and a cup of coffee from morning to night.

There is not much time to think of one's soul when the body cries out for food. "You cannot preach the gospel to men with empty stomachs," Abbé Lugan says.

So we make our plea for houses of hospitality which in the shadow of the church recall men to Christ and to the job of rebuilding the social order. Catholic France had 2,000 leper houses during that time of emergency in the Middle Ages. We are confronted by an emergency today, a need that only Christians can supply. We must bring workers to Christ as it has been done down through the ages and is being done today in all missionary lands.

Tale of Two Capitals 9

1939 sees no end to human misery in the United States. Here are reports from Washington and Harrisburg.

Washington

It is a hot summer afternoon in Washington, but there is a good breeze coming in the windows as I write. The radio is going in the front room—soothing waltzes—and Mary is sitting in a flowered voile dress embroidering a doily. Mary is quite black and her dress is very fresh and white, and she is a picture, cool and calm. She has set the two big tables for supper, which is her share of the evening's work. She and her two sisters have also helped me to peel potatoes in the back yard. The beans have been strung and Miss Selew has seared the meat and it is now simmering away in a deep pan, covered with good brown gravy. Betty Walsh soon comes in from her classes at the Catholic University to finish up the job and serve.

Originally published in *Commonweal* 30 (July 14, 1939): 288–90.

It is her turn, but she has been giving an examination, so everyone had jumped into the breach.

Dinner is served at Il Poverello House on Tenth Street in Washington every night at six-thirty, and swarms of the children of the neighborhood come in. There are three little girls living in the house and two big girls, both graduates of Francis Xavier University in New Orleans, now finishing up a year of graduate work at the Catholic University. These, with the two older women, who teach at the University, make up the family.

But everyone in the neighborhood considers the house a sort of headquarters and comes for aid of one kind or another. The doors are open when the women get home from school and the work of hospitality goes on. Bedtime is early, because everyone gets up at quarter past five to offer the Mass at the shrine at quarter of six, where they all make the responses together, and where Father Paul Hanley Furfey gives a short homily every day. It's a good way of starting the day, and the early morning is cool and fragrant as we drive over to the shrine.

The life of the group at Il Poverello house is dedicated to voluntary poverty. The principle is, "If we have less, everyone will have more." So on this very immediate practical idea, many are helped.

They certainly need help, the Negroes in Washington. Down the alley in back of this house—it is a two-story, box-like structure for which the rent is $75 a month—the tiny little houses with no running water, rent for $16 a month. Quite literally they are hovels. Places that would rent for $8 a month in New York cost twice as much here. And places are hard to find.

Washington is a beautiful city; the streets are tree-shaded and on the streets the houses are mostly not bad. But down the alleys live the great mass of poor, crowded in dirty, evil-smelling, little holes. There the unemployed hang out, dull and lethargic, some vicious and dissipated, as well as the greater number who struggle against terrific odds to keep themselves human, to rise above their surroundings.

The Blessed Martin Home

Down at 1215 Seventh Street, Llewellyn Scott manages his house of hospitality which he calls the Blessed Martin Home. The address is on Seventh Street but the entrance is down the alley. On the door hangs a crucifix. The stairs leading to the two floors above a barber shop are dark and rickety. On the walls are holy pictures and in the two sitting rooms upstairs are many more. There are beds everywhere, even in the front living room, which is filled with books and some easy chairs. In this room a very old man sleeps.

"I don't like to put him in with the others; they get to talking and arguing and make him nervous," Llewellyn said. "The other night two of them in the other sitting room were arguing about what they had been able to see out of their jail windows at Leavenworth and they were getting wild. I had to go in and shush them. I never have any trouble and nobody ever gets rough. In the three years I've been running the place, we've never had the police in."

Llewellyn Scott is a colored man who works part time for the government. Out of his salary he supports an aged mother and an invalid sister: pays their rent, which is partly covered by two roomers, and feeds them. He uses the rest of his meager resources to keep the Blessed Martin House going. During the past year he has served 17,780 meals and during the winter he put up about forty-five men a night. Today there were fifteen men sleeping in the house, as many as the beds could hold.

The place is terribly dilapidated. Paper hangs from the walls, and underneath the plaster has fallen off and the slats show. The floor slopes in every direction and you walk up and down a grade as you go from room to room. The rent is $26 a month. It is unheated, and in winter they can afford only two gallons of oil a day to try to keep it warm. Down on the first floor in what was originally a big storeroom, he has made a chapel and lined it with corrugated cardboard. There an altar is set up with a statue of the Sacred Heart. Today there were flowers in front of it, peonies and dahlias. They had spent twenty-five cents which a woman had given them (they had been praying for her sick daughter)—money which they might have spent for food. There are plenty of chairs in the chapel and four prie-dieux. Here at five-thirty every night they gather for the rosary and the litany. Most of the men who come to the place are not Catholics, but they soon learn the prayers and they all love to sing.

"The Board of Health came and made me take out some of the beds," Llewellyn said. "They wanted to know if I had a covered garbage can. I told them garbage cans were for rich folks. We have nothing to throw away. When we have nothing we don't eat. But down the street a Jewish baker gives us bread."

John J. O'Brien, veteran, sat with us there as we talked. On the window sill a tiny black kitten washed itself with a bright pink tongue. John had just hiked down from Chester, Pennsylvania. He had been in Philadelphia, visiting the Catholic Worker house there, and he talked of the conditions in Chester. Fifteen hundred men just thrown out of work by a factory which was moving south, and a few hundred men just let off a ship. We ought to start a place there.

John started a place here in Washington recently but it only lasted two months. He started with too much rent, $45 a month, which he paid out of money he had saved from his small pension. He had visited the place in Pittsburgh and it was there he got the idea. Houses of hospitality for men all over the country. Using all the unoccupied buildings. The men building up self-help groups, working together for mutual aid.

His place didn't last because John became terrified. Convents and monasteries started sending him their mendicants and he was not able to handle them all. He didn't know how to feed them, how to live from day to day. He didn't know that Saint Joseph is supposed to handle those things for us. He had expected that human agencies would step in and help once the thing got started, and when no one came to help he got discouraged.

Last month the house closed up and he passed on the furniture to Llewellyn. Now, however, he is determined to start again, this time with a smaller place and expecting nothing. "I'll do what I can myself, and I'm not going to stop. I'm going to keep after this. I'll start now the little way."

It's a strange fight for the weather-bitten veteran, clad in dungarees, used to the roads and the men who are tramping the roads. It's a new kind of a fight, but something has to be done.

"We'll do what we can," he repeated, "and some day they'll take these unoccupied buildings and start some hospices. A place to live and something to eat now, and then we can plan on what to do. Then we can plan on getting back the land."

Harrisburg

All the Catholic Worker houses of hospitality aim to be poor. They are in the slums but somehow we never get down quite low enough. There are always a few rungs lower to go on the ladder of destitution. Besides when we get through scrubbing and painting or whitewashing, there is a decent look about the houses which contrasts greatly with other places in the neighborhood. Llewellyn Scott's place in Washington is poverty stricken and dilapidated beyond hope of repair. The building just won't stand it. The house in Philadelphia has an outside toilet, a shanty in back, but, unlike other places in the neighborhood, at least it is not one to be shared with five other houses.

Here in Harrisburg there just isn't any toilet. You go next door to the neighbors. And there was no running water until a week ago. Most of the houses on the block have no running water. The neighbors pay one man down the street for the privilege of getting pails of water from his house.

Our place, the Blessed Martin Home, is two rooms, now scrubbed clean. There is electricity, tables and chairs, magazines to read. There is paint and linoleum on the floor, the linoleum donated out of her salary by a colored cook who works all day and then comes over to help us in the evening.

There is a faucet in the kitchen now, but no sink. We are begging for that.

The women, colored and white, who are engaging in the Catholic Worker activities among the children and families in the neighborhood, are supporting themselves and there is little money to spare. They have to advance little by little, at a snail's pace.

Due to lack of decent living facilities, no one is resident in the house permanently, but different families have been given the use of the place as a temporary lodging—two white families with thirteen and seven children respectively and one colored family with seven children.

How they got along in two rooms with no water and no toilet is hard to understand. But these families had been evicted in the quiet, orderly way Harrisburg, capital of Pennsylvania, has of doing such things. A moving van drives up to the door, the furniture is carted out and put in storage. The family is turned into the streets to roam around until some welfare agency or relief bureau takes the case up and resettles them. Then they pay for moving into their next place. In one case the children were rolled out of bed and left in their night things as the clothes and bedding were loaded on the van. Even the ice box with some food in it was taken. Neighbors sheltered the evicted family.

Our house sheltered Lucille, too. Lucille was a colored girl, twenty-three years old. She was found dying in an empty house by Mary Frecon, who is our Harrisburg representative. Lucille grew up on the streets. She and her brothers and sisters just prowled around, living as best they could. For the last few months, ravaged with syphilis and drink, Lucille had been cared for by an old colored man who lived in an abandoned shed down an alley. He gave her his cot—that and a chair were the only things he had—and he waited on her as best he could. But the flies were eating her alive, huge horse flies, and in her agony she crawled out and sought shade and relief in an abandoned house next to ours where another old colored man had taken refuge. He too took care of her—they know the uselessness of appealing to agencies—until the neighbors told Mary about it. She found her moaning and crying and trying to beat away the flies that fastened themselves on her open sores.

The few women who carry on the Catholic Worker activities here brought her into their clean little rooms and there they tried to take care of her.

Not a hospital in Harrisburg would have her and it was only after five days that Dr. Boland got an ambulance from Steelton (they could not get one at Harrisburg) and sent her to the House of the Good Shepherd at Philadelphia where they deposited her without a word and with no papers about her case. The House of the Good Shepherd is not a hospital, but it is for such girls as Lucille had been. So they took her in, nursed her, and there she died not many weeks later.

While she was lying over in the Catholic Worker house she had been baptized and anointed by Father Kirchner of St. Patrick's Cathedral.

Harrisburg is full of Lucilles and a few visits to the slums there can explain why.

After we visited the children and some of the neighbors at 1019 Seventh Street tonight, we went across the street to Mrs. Wright. She lives in a rickety two-storied house, owned by the city and completely out of repair. The banisters are falling down and the steps are unsafe. Here in the only two habitable rooms, she, her seven children, her husband and another woman have refuge. They have three beds and they all sleep in one room. The kitchen is only big enough for the stove, the table and a few chairs.

Mrs. Wright sat there with her youngest baby, six months old, on her lap. He is thin and moans constantly. He has had pneumonia and whooping cough, one house burned down around him and the other day the whole ceiling came down upon his crib. He has lived through these six months, but from the look of him he will not live much longer, poor baby. And God knows he will be happier dead. It is hard to see the look of settled sadness on the faces of the others.

Mary Frecon and Jean Records tried to clean the place up for them. They went in with pails and mops and with cold water and plenty of soap they scrubbed and scoured. But it didn't show. The hot foul air caught at our throats as we went in, and half strangled us.

Mary Frecon, married and with a family to look after, is not able to live in the house of hospitality at Harrisburg, but she has certainly made her home another CW unit. Right now she has a young woman with two small babies, one and three years old, living with her. She picked them up at one of the evictions she was covering. The girl's husband has abandoned her and she has endured great hardships. There were even nights before her second baby was born that she sat out on doorsteps all night. For the last year or so she had been making her home with other poor families and working for them.

The greatest difficulty in Harrisburg is to find a home to live in, even when a family is on relief and has money to pay rent. Housing seems to be the greatest immediate problem of the city. But thanks to Mary Frecon and the Harrisburg Housing Association which she has built up (it is an interracial group) there is now $1,800,000 available for housing projects and half of it is going for the Negro. Not much, but something to start on. Mary is interested in projects which will enable the residents to have land where they can raise their own food, but it will take a great fight to put that over. But she is a fighter, and we are hoping that her efforts will see to it that this new housing is for the truly poor and not just for middle-class salaried workers, as it usually is.

It Was a Good Dinner   **10**

Summer in the city is hard, particularly in poor neighborhoods

In summer it is hard. Everybody goes away on vacations and those who can't go away are sending others away. Students have finished paying expenses for one year and are looking forward to paying expenses for another year at school. Nobody has any money, especially those who want to help, who are the most generous.

I don't know how we could make out if it were not for the free vegetables we are getting this summer. Free rolls and cakes too. We go on charging our coffee, sugar and milk, and a great supply of bread, 250 pounds a day. And of course we have to buy meat. Once in a while we can get a supply of fish from the Fulton Market, a barrelful at a time, and then the cleaning takes place in the backyard, and if it is fish with roe in it we fry up the roe and there is an afternoon tea party with fish-roe sandwiches, everybody prowling around like cats, licking their chops.

Originally published in *Commonweal* 32 (August 23, 1940): 364–65.

It is fun cleaning the fish in the courtyard between the houses. A long table is brought out and everybody who can find a knife joins in. We have to cook the entire barrelful and everyone has to eat as much as he can. It would be dangerous to keep it, as our icebox never seems to get very cold. The difficulty is to get fat to fry the fish. It takes a lot of lard to fry a barrelful. But oh, the smell while it is cooking! It is enough to reconcile one to the other smells which hang over the backyard for a few days after.

Meat is a scarcity, however. Once this summer we had a ham which a kind friend brought in, and even slicing it very small it was hard to make it go round to one hundred and twenty-five people. None of the fellows who were cooking in the kitchen had any. I came up at the tail end of the dinner. Stanley Vishnewski had finished the spiritual reading, "In the Footsteps of Saint Francis," and was sitting down to a meatless plate. The boys had saved a piece for me and there was applesauce and mashed potatoes besides. Oblivious to Stanley's lack I was digging in with great enjoyment.

And then there came a wail from the kitchen. "No meat for me? And I've been working all day! I don't see how everybody else rates meat, and not me. Those that hang around and do nothing get the best food, and me, I went on an errand and so I get left."

The querulous tones went on. The fellow came in, looking sadly at his plate; slammed it on the table and sat down. "I been smelling that all afternoon, too. I just *wanted* a piece of ham."

I offered him half of mine, Ed Kelleher, who used to be a house detective, and a gentle, holy soul he is, too, offered him his.

"I don't eat off nobody's plate," the hungry one said. "But I did want a piece of that ham." A great tear rolled down his nose.

It is incidents like this that break your heart, sometimes. There is never enough food to go around. The pots are always being scraped so clean it is a wonder the enamel doesn't come off. There never is anything in the Electrolux ice box we bought for fifty dollars from the baker around the corner, five dollars down and five dollars once in a while. He gives us a lot of free bread and rolls, too.

Meals are so important. The disciples knew Christ in the breaking of bread. We know Christ in each other in the breaking of bread. It is the closest we can ever come to each other, sitting down and eating together. It is unbelievably, poignantly intimate.

A good supper

Last night we had a very good supper. John Kernan and Duncan Chisholm have charge of the kitchen and Shorty is the *sous-chef*. They also have as assistants John Monaghan and Jim O'Hearn. They take charge of the lunch and dinner every day, and another staff, under Peter Clark, takes charge of the eight hundred on the bread line each morning. These hot days nobody wants anything but bread and coffee, and the bread is pumpernickel or rye, good and substantial. I read some place, I think it was in one of these ten-cent-store children's books on "Wheat," that the gluten in wheat is the nearest thing to human flesh. And it was wheat that Christ chose when He left us His presence on our altars!

Lunch is always simple, a huge vegetable soup and bread. We make about twenty gallons, and it does a thorough job of heating the kitchen these broiling days.

Supper is more elaborate—sometimes we say "dinner." Last week, thanks to a Long Island farmer and the priest who sent him to us, we had a good vegetable supper—potatoes, beets, carrots, cabbage. We had to buy the potatoes off him at seventy-five cents a bushel, but the rest came free. By Sunday we had run out of cabbage and carrots so we had potatoes and beets. As it was Sunday, we had got fifteen pounds of chopped meat, at fifteen cents a pound, and made a meat loaf. There was a goodly amount of bread mixed with it.

Gravies

John is a genius at making gravies. I doubt the Waldorf-Astoria has better gravies than we do. It was so good a meal, and everybody was so hungry, not having eaten all day, what with the heat, that I became consumed with anxiety as to whether the food was going to stretch for all. The back court seemed to be full of men and women and there were even some children. One woman had walked all the way down from Fifteenth Street with her two-year-old to have a hot meal. Her gas and electric had been turned off and she could not cook. She is on relief and never seems to catch up, she says.

Little Billy ran around the dining room disrupting things between bites, so we moved mother and child out to the kitchen to finish their meal so the line could go on. We can't seat more than twenty-five and there have to be six sittings. I had finished early and begun hovering over the pots on the stove. John kept counting the men on the line. "Thirty-six more to go," he groaned as he sliced down the last of the meat loaf. Soon he was putting the scraps in the gravy and began contemplating that.

"Get me the gravy-stretcher," he called to Shorty; and Shorty, always willing, began to scurry about the kitchen, proffering him one utensil after another. (I one day asked Shorty if he had any relatives, and he said mournfully, "I had a mother once.")

Finally it dawned on him that it was a bit more hot water John wanted to stretch the gravy with, and he brought it. Then a bowlful of boiled potatoes was discovered and they were peeled and dumped into the frying pans. John believes in having things nice.

"Eighteen left to go," Monaghan said as he leaned out the window and looked. And then suddenly five more women, from the Salvation Army hotel on Rivington Street, came in and threw our calculations out again. (Women are always served first and the men step to one side to let them get by.)

"Eight more coming up," and by this time the mashed potatoes were gone and fried potatoes were being dished up.

Thank God there was still plenty of good gravy, and there were some chunks of meat in it too. Not a speck came back on the plates. They were all wiped clean with bits of bread.

And then the last one was served, and there was exactly one helping left! The dishes were being done as we went along, the pots were all cleaned, and there remained only the tables to swab off and the kitchen and dining room to sweep, and we were done.

The one helping was put away in the icebox (and Julia came in around ten and had not eaten since lunch); and then everyone went out of the hot house to the street, where all the neighbors sit in rows along the house-fronts and along the curb and there are card games going on all the long evening.

Down the street the children had turned on a fire hydrant and flung a barrel over it, a headless barrel, and the water cascaded into the air thirty feet like a fountain. The sound was pleasant and so were the cheers of the children as they rushed through the deluge. Little boys paddled "boats" in the rushing curb-streams. Shopkeepers deflected the water onto their sidewalks and began sweeping, and mothers moved their baby carriages out of the flood. All the little boys and some of the little girls got their feet soaked.

Down the street came a singer with his accordion and the happy sound of Italian love songs accompanied the rushing sound of our sudden city streams.

John and Jim of the kitchen sat and rested and there was a look of happy content on their faces. They are both jobless, and are volunteers in the work of our Catholic Worker Community; there is war in the world and they are faced with conscription and little else in the way of security for the future. But it was a fine happy evening and it had been a very good meal.

About Mary
11

This morning after Communion I thought of writing about Mary, and since the thought came to me at *that* time, I took it as an order.

I always say to the Blessed Mother after Communion—"Here He is in my heart; I believe, help thou mine unbelief; adore Him, thank Him and love Him for me. He is your Son; His honor is in your hands. Do not let me dishonor Him."

And since too at that moment came this thought, those glimpses of all she has meant to me—all the little contacts with her that brought me to Him—I felt I must write.

One of the reasons I do not write more is that there is always housework, cleaning, scrubbing, sewing, washing (right now it is cleaning fish), etc., to do. Just as she had to do these things, and probably never neglected them. But then too I can see her sitting seemingly idle beside a well on just such a day as this, just thanking Him, with each happy breath.

പ്ര

Originally published in *Commonweal* 39 (November 5, 1943): 62–63.

Down in New Orleans twenty years ago I was working for the *Item*, an afternoon paper, and the job was not a very satisfactory one. Women writers, "girl reporters," had to write feature stuff. I started in writing a column about homely things—the same kind of a column I write now— the "Day after Day" column, in *The Catholic Worker*. But they soon gave me assignments, some good, some bad. I had to interview Jack Dempsey, and such like, visiting celebrities. Once I had to cover the political situation and write a series of interviews with the retiring governor and the newly-elected governor of the state. I had to work in a dance hall for a week as a taxi dancer and write a series of articles, in one of which I insulted, so they said, the United States Navy. Representatives from the sailors of a battleship in port at the time came to the newspaper office to rebuke me. It was a change from the work I had been doing in Chicago in the radical movement. But I didn't like it much.

Across the street from where I lived, I think it was on St. Peter Street, there was the side entrance to the cathedral. Every night I used to go in there for Benediction. Perhaps I was influenced by reading the novels of Huysmans that I had borrowed from Sam Putnam's library in Chicago. My roommate was Mary Gordon (when I last heard of her, she was working for the League for Spanish Democracy in Chicago, a Communist affiliate), and that Christmas she gave me a rosary. So in this case I was led to the Church through two Communists. I did not know how to say the rosary, but I got a little prayer book at a Catholic book store which I often visited, and I learned how. Once in a while I said it. I remember expressing the desire to talk to a priest—to the girl who ran the book shop—but nothing came of it.

໖

My first statue of the Blessed Mother. Peggy was my roommate in jail in Washington. When we were in the Occoquan workhouse we had adjoining rooms. In the Washington city jail I had the upper berth on one of the upper tiers, and Peggy had the lower. I read the Bible and she wrote a book of poetry—"Poems to My

Lovers," she called it. I also read letters from the boys I was going with at the time, one of them, my most regular correspondent, a United States sailor. It was during the last war. Some years afterward Peggy gave me a little statue of the Blessed Mother which had been brought from Czechoslovakia. It was made of wax, and very delicate, and there was a golden watchspring-like halo around its head, and golden curly hair and a bright blue robe. How I loved that statue! Down in Staten Island in my little shore cottage I kept it on a shelf by the door with a vigil light burning in front of it.

Peggy also was a member of the Communist party at different times, but being an undisciplined creature and an artist I don't think she was a paid-up member for long.

ↄↄ

One summer right after I became a Catholic I was taking care of a number of little boys from a school "for individual development." Together with Freda, my next-door neighbor, whose friend it was who ran the school, we took the responsibility for about a dozen boys between eight and twelve. Quite a few of them were children of Communist parents, and several of them have grown up now to be members of the Young Communist League. I used to read them the "Little Flowers of Saint Francis," which they enjoyed immensely, and they used to command each other "in the name of holy obedience" to perform this or that act of mischief. They also used to ask me to burn candles for them before the little blue statue of the Blessed Mother. Do any of them remember her now?

ↄↄ

When my daughter was born almost eighteen years ago, I turned her over to the Blessed Mother. "What kind of a mother am I going to be?" I kept thinking to myself. "What kind of a Catholic home is she going to have, with only me?" And with the Catholic Worker movement starting six years later the home problem was even more acute.

There was a solution of course to such a difficulty. "You," I told the Blessed Mother, "will have to be her mother. Under the best of circumstances I'm a failure as a homemaker. I'm untidy, inconsistent, undisciplined, temperamental, and I have to pray hard every day for final perseverance."

It is only these last few years that it has occurred to me why my daughter has never called me "mother." From the time she first spoke, it was "Dorothy." I'd think—"of course with no other children around calling me 'mother' it is natural for her to call me by my first name." I'd correct her but it did no good. Later on I'd ask her, "How will anyone know I'm your mother if you do not call me 'mother'? They'll think I adopted you. They'll think I'm your aunt or something." "I don't care," she would say firmly, "I just can't call you 'mother.'" And for a child really extremely obedient, it was hard to understand such stubbornness.

Once, in the little post office on Staten Island—she was four then—the postmistress said, "I'd like to hear a child of mine call me by my first name! I'd give it to her!"

When she was in convent school her brief letters began *"Dear Mother,"* but it was under compulsion. The Sisters would not let her write unless she so began. But away from school, the letters continue, "Dear Dorothy."

And then a few years ago, it came like a flash of light, "The Blessed Virgin Mary is Mother of my child."

The Scandal of the Works of Mercy 12

To reach the man in the street you must go to the street, where Christianity itself may be a sign of contradiction.

The spiritual works of mercy are: to admonish the sinner, to instruct the ignorant, to counsel the doubtful, to comfort the sorrowful, to bear wrongs patiently, to forgive all injuries, and to pray for the living and the dead.

The corporal works are to feed the hungry, to give drink to the thirsty, to clothe the naked, to ransom the captive, to harbor the harborless, to visit the sick, and to bury the dead.

When Peter Maurin talked about the necessity of practicing the works of mercy, he meant all of them, and he envisioned houses of hospitality in poor parishes in every city of the country, where these precepts of Our Lord could be put into effect. He pointed out that we have turned to State responsibility through home relief, social legislation and social security, and we no longer practice personal responsibility for our brother, but are repeating the words of the first murderer, "Am I my brother's keeper?" Not that our passing the buck is as crude as all that. It

Originally published in *Commonweal* 51 (November 4, 1949): 99–102.

was a matter of social enlightenment, Holy Mother the City taking over, Holy Mother the State taking the poor to herself, gathering them to her capacious bosom studded with the jewels of the taxation of the rich and the poor alike, the subtle war between Church and State meanwhile going on at all times, in the field of education, charity, the family. In the last fifteen years the all-encroaching State, as the Bishops of the United States have called it, has gained the upper hand.

In our fight against such a concept of Christian charity, we have been accused of lining up with Wall Street and private enterprise, and the rich opponents of state control and taxation. But, anarchists that we are, we want to decentralize everything and delegate to smaller bodies and groups what can be done far more humanly and responsibly through mutual aid, as well as charity, through Blue Cross, Red Cross, union cooperation, parish cooperation.

Peter Maurin, the founder of the Catholic Worker, was very much an apostle to the world today, not only to the poor. He was a prophet with a social message and he wanted to reach the people with it. To get to the people, he pointed out it was necessary to embrace voluntary poverty, to strip yourself, which would give you the means to practice the works of mercy. To reach the man in the street you must go to the street. To reach the workers, you begin to study a philosophy of labor, and take up manual labor, useful labor, instead of white collar work. To be the least, to be the worker, to be poor, to take the lowest place and thus be the spark which would set afire the love of men towards each other and to God (and we can only show our love for God by our love for our fellows). These were Peter's ideas, and they are indispensable for the performing of the works of mercy.

When Father Lombardi spoke a few weeks ago in St. Patrick's Cathedral and on the Fordham campus, he spoke of the need to make a new social order. He was making no anti-Communist speech, he said. He was making no nationalist speech. He was speaking a gospel of love, and that meant here and now a redistribution of this world's goods, so that a man could have as many children as God sent him, and support them, have a home for them and work for them to do. This world's goods do not belong to any one nation, any few men, he pointed out.

෨

We are all devoured by a passion for social justice today, and seeking an alternative to communism and capitalism. We like to discuss capitalism, industrialism, distributism, decentralization—all the work that is being done by the National Catholic Welfare Conference in Washington and by the National Catholic Rural Life Conference, but with this tremendous work of indoctrination, with all this work which goes on in conference, convention, classroom, and through periodicals, much of it comes to words and not very vital words at that.

Peter liked to talk of making a message dynamic, and that meant with him putting it into practice. There was simple common sense in his argument that if you wanted to reach the man in the street, you go out on a park bench with him, you go out to sell your paper on the street just as the Jehovah's Witnesses do, just as the Communists do.

Publishing a paper and reaching the man in the street, was to Peter, performing the first four of the spiritual works of mercy. To go on picket lines, was to perform spiritual works of mercy. It was to dramatize by a supplicatory procession the needs of the worker, the injustice perpetrated against him. To bear wrongs patiently, yes, but not to let the bosses continue in the sin of exploiting you. To forgive the injury, yes, but to try to do away with the injury.

I remember one time when we were all picketing in the National Biscuit Company strike on West Fourteenth Street. There was a mass picket line which extended around the block, and the police began to break it up, and then the scabs arrived in taxi cabs and the mob started to boo, and the whole affair began to look ugly. As we gave out our literature, Frank O'Donnell, who is now one of the members of the farming community at St. Benedict's Farm at Upton, Mass., turned to us all and said mildly, winking at Peter, "Don't forget we are all gentle personalities!"

It reminded me of the Communist who shouted at me as we were dispersed by the police at another demonstration, and there was a brutal show of force by the police: "What about a little brotherly love, sister?"

Yes, such works of mercy, such spiritual works of mercy, can be dangerous, and can smack of class war attitudes. And of that we are often accused, because the performance of the works of mercy finds us on the side of the poor, the exploited, whether with literature, picketing, soup kitchen, etc. As Evelyn Waugh said to us plaintively last spring, "Don't you think the rich suffer too?"

∽

We are always accused of going to extremes and perhaps it does seem like an extreme to be talking of the street apostolate and the retreat apostolate in the same breath. Yet they go together. In the attempt to perform these works of mercy, which are far more difficult than the immediate physical ones of feeding and clothing and sheltering, we came to the decision after ten years of work in city and country throughout the land that we needed a retreat house for the work. We had had colloquiums for the clarification of thought, and tired of wrangling, we had tried an annual retreat for all the leaders of the Catholic Worker Houses in the United States; so many came, and the response was so great, that we decided to have a year-round retreat house where we could raise what we needed as much as possible, where we could build up our very good library, where we could have a house of studies for those who wanted to stay longer than the week's retreat on the farm.

The first project was at Easton, and never was there such a retreat house. Generous priests gave us their time, and came and slept in unheated rooms and dormitories. At first there was no running water, but one valiant priest, Father Pacifique Roy, S.S.J., who had been a missionary both in Quebec and Louisiana and accustomed to working with his hands, directed the work by example as well as by precept, and we dug ditches and laid pipe and soon had running water on every floor of the barn and the house. We had electricity in every room, and the electrical work was done by Father Roy and our men. During the war, when it was all but impossible to get men or materials, we had the genius of this priest who knew how to use all odds and ends of pipe and wire and make up gadgets to take the place of those we could not get. If Father Roy could have been spared to us (he is invalided in Canada right now) we would have had a lumber mill, a cement block plant and a grist mill and electricity from our own windmill, and all such contrivances of human ingenuity for our farm retreat house.

As it is, we have become more bourgeois and comfortable, but not more self-sufficient. We have a long way to go to exemplify the poverty of a St. Francis or a Peter Maurin.

People out of jails and out of hospitals, men from the breadline and from the road, readers of the paper from all walks of life, students, priests too, come to make retreats with us. We have a chapel in which the stations of the cross, the statues of the Blessed Mother and St. Joseph are made by our own artists. Adé de Bethune carved the crucifix over the altar, and the altar and the benches were made by one of the men who came in from the Bowery, an old carpenter with a bitter tongue, who so despised the unskilled poor that whenever anyone gave any evidence of any skill, he would say sourly, "And what jail did you learn that in?"

This old man nearing eighty had his little shop and house right at the entrance to our farm at Easton, where we first had retreats, and unlike the porter at the gate described by St. Benedict, old Maurice had quite a different tongue. I used to feel sad that instead of seeing Christ in each guest who came, he saw the bum, and so treated us, one and all. He was a good example of "The Friend of the Family," "The Man Who Came to Dinner." And also a fitting member of our community, which is country-wide by now, and which Stanley Vishnewski has come to call "the *contemptibles*." "It is a new order I started," he is going around saying. But it is really Peter Maurin who started it. Stanley just named it.

Our retreat house now is at Newburgh, New York, sixty-five miles up the Hudson River. . . . We are intending to sell [it] and buy one on some bay near New York where we can fish and so cut down our expenses. . . .

ତ୬

It will be seen that our concept of the works of mercy, including as it does making the kind of society where the "rich man becomes poor, and the poor holy," a society where there is no unemployment, and where each can "work according to his ability and receive according to his need," is a foretaste of heaven indeed.

. . . We have daily Mass at the Farm, and we are permitted by the Chancery Office to have the Blessed Sacrament at all times while a priest is with us and we are blessed in having an invalided priest visiting us these past fifteen months or so. We have Prime and Compline, we have sung Masses for all the big feast days, we have readings at the table during retreats, and sometimes when there is no retreat but a feast day to be celebrated. There are many visitors, and it is very much a crowded inn and hospice during all the months of the year. . . .

There are families among us who do not have much time for many of the works of mercy any longer outside their own families, though they are always contributors of food and clothing to our community of contemptibles. And it is indeed true that there are many celibates, willing and unwilling ones, among us. Converts come to work with us who might have preferred family life but are barred from it by a previous bad marriage. There will always be, in a way, the willing and the reluctant celibates, and for these, the community life of the Catholic Worker, with its men and women working together, dedicated to the common effort, affords the comfort of a home, of contacts with friends, the normal, happy relationships of men and women working together. (The men become more gentle and the women try harder to please, and in spite of the war of sexes which goes on and always will, there is a growth of the good love of friendship so sadly needed in the world today.)

❧

The works of mercy are a wonderful stimulus to our growth in faith as well as in love. Our faith is taxed to the utmost and so grows through this strain put upon it. It is pruned again and again, and springs up bearing much fruit. For anyone starting to live literally the words of the Fathers of the Church, "the bread you retain belongs to the hungry, the dress you lock up is the property of the naked," "what is superfluous for one's need is to be regarded as plunder if one retains it for one's self," there is always a trial ahead. "Our faith, more precious than gold, must be tried as though by fire." Here is a letter we received today. "I took a gentleman seemingly in need of spiritual and temporal guidance into my home on a Sunday afternoon. Let him have a nap on my bed, went through the want ads with him, made coffee and sandwiches for him, and when he left, I found my wallet had gone also."

I can only say that the Saints would only bow their heads and not try to understand or judge. They received no thanks—well then, God had to repay them. They forebore to judge, and it was as though they took off their cloak besides their coat to give away. This is expecting heroic charity of course. But these things happen for our discouragement, for our testing. We are sowing the seed of love, and we are not living in the harvest time so that we can expect a crop. We must love to the point of folly, and we are indeed fools, as our Lord Himself was who died for such a one as this. We lay down our lives too when we have performed so painfully thankless an act, because this correspondent of ours is poor in this world's goods. It is agony to go through such bitter experiences, because we all want to love, we desire with a great longing to love our fellows, and our hearts are often crushed at such rejections. But a Carmelite nun said to me last week, "It is the crushed heart which is the soft heart, the tender heart," and maybe it is one way to become meek and humble of heart like Jesus.

. . . Well, our friend has suffered from his experience and it is part of the bitterness of the poor, who cheat each other, who exploit each other, even as they are exploited. Who despise each other even as they are the despised.

And is it to be expected that virtue and destitution should go together? No, as John Cogley has written, they are the destitute in every way, destitute of this world's goods, destitute of honor, of gratitude, of love, and they need so much, that we cannot take the works of mercy apart, and say I will do this one, or that one work of mercy. We find they all go together.

Some years ago there was an article in *Commonweal* by Georges Bernanos. He ended his article as I shall end mine, paraphrasing his words, and it is a warning note for these apocalyptic times: "Every particle of Christ's divine charity is today more precious for your security—for your security, I say—than all the atom bombs in all the stock piles." It is by the works of mercy that we shall be judged.

Traveling by Bus   13

You can see the country, meet the people . . . and get where you're going at half the price.

Where do you get all the money to travel around with?" is one of the embarrassing questions asked us when we appear on lecture platforms, and it is asked also in letters from some of the readers of *The Catholic Worker* who disagree with the positions we take. They want to let us know they are judging us severely for spending money, which should go to the poor, on jaunting over the highways.

If we write on poverty, and we shall continue to do so, and have others write such articles for *The Catholic Worker* from month to month, it is necessary to meet such questions.

It shows how seriously our readers and listeners take this call to poverty, holy poverty, voluntary poverty, which is the foundation, the starting point of all our work for man's freedom, his dignity and for his love.

Originally published in *Commonweal* 51 (March 10, 1950): 577–79.

Let us say that travel by bus is traveling in poverty but not in destitution. It costs about half as much as by railroad. And as people say who are doing it for the first time, and think they have lowered their standards a little, "you see so much of the country."

I have just returned from a trip to the West Coast, half of which was made by bus. Now that the war is over, you do not have to make reservations ahead but can go to the stations half an hour early and get your tickets. The Greyhound of course is the best. The Trailways bus is so built that there is no room for the knees. I have spent a night of misery between New York and Washington, wedged in at the side of a stout woman and with the seat ahead pressing close against me.

Between our farm at Newburgh and New York there are two bus lines operating, the Short Line and the Mohawk. The latter has the more comfortable buses, with reclining seats. But it follows the thrilling, somewhat terrifying road which winds around Bear Mountain and Storm King Mountain. The road is clearly labeled "Dangerous but Passable" and is posted with signs, "Falling Rocks," which cause you to peer up at the jagged cliffs hanging overhead, while you shudder away from the abyss on the other side. The Short Line follows the less picturesque truck route.

There are no dangers between here and the Rockies on the cross-country trip, if you leave out of account fog, sleet and the snow storms at this time of the year. In winter the buses are more crowded because no one can use cars. Between all the little villages along the route people crowd into the buses, smelling of fresh air and snow and talking of conditions back off the highway, of the trucks that are stalled ahead and behind. Just when the radio is warning drivers to keep off the roads I feel safest, because then the cars crawl along and there are fewer of them. I really feel secure in the heavy vehicle that I could never conceivably drive myself, so I don't even have the back-seat driver tendencies that I have in other cars.

We had a good driver leaving New York, cheerful and informative. As we went through the Holland Tunnel he told his passengers all about the explosion which took place in the tunnel some months before. We held our breath, praying, until we got through. Going over the Pulaski Skyway, he said, "This is seven miles long, it took seven years to build, and it cost seven men their lives."

I had heard the same comment about the Golden Gate Bridge. How many lives were lost on these roads, these bridges and tunnels which common men built and dug! You cannot travel by bus without having these ideas impressed upon you, up through the all but impenetrable canyons where power lines have been carried, pipe has been laid, roads have been built, if not stone by stone as in Roman times then actually foot by foot of slow and daily progress from one end of this vast country to the other. It makes you more patient with the slow work you are doing, the small job, the making of meals, the giving out of clothes, the building of that bridge of love from man to man, the creation of a sense of community, fellowship.

This first bus driver stayed with us to Binghamton, I believe, and he was kindly all the way. He allowed plenty of time for rest stops, and counted his passengers whenever he started out again. People have sometimes been left behind by surly bus drivers. One such driver can set the tone of the whole trip, making people grumble and snap at each other. There may be a chain reaction in the mood of the busload, going from the driver to the passengers.

We had one such driver from Chicago to St. Louis, but we found toward the close of the trip that he was suffering from an abscess on the base of his spine and that he could not lay off work to get it attended to, especially around holiday time. Indeed, at the stop where someone was supposed to relieve him, the other driver did not show up, and he was forced to take the bus on into St. Louis. The bus was an old rattletrap affair that was only put on the route over the holidays. The heater did not work, and one could comfort oneself only by thinking of the stagecoach of Dickens's day. The poor driver was so ill he got out at every stop to be sick, and, though he stopped five or ten minutes, he always snarled at us all that it was not a rest stop, we were not to leave the bus. Towards the close of the evening he broke down and confessed to us all how sick he felt; then he went on with the account of his woe to two men sitting in back of him. He told them of all his troubles with his wife and his mother-in-law. They returned his confidences.

 〇

Sometimes bus passengers are not the pleasantest of companions. Once in a great while you are afflicted with someone who is a bore and, very rarely, with a real nuisance. I had one such experience in Texas riding from Amarillo to Phoenix. My sufferings became so acute that I had to get off in Albuquerque and wait for the next bus. The problem was an elderly minister (he showed me his card) who confessed that he was running away from his responsibilities. To bolster his courage, he got off at every stop and had a few drinks. I had been visiting a Negro woman in Amarillo who packed me a most elaborate lunch with some delicious roast beef sandwiches. It would have been rude, of course, to eat alone, so I had offered one of the sandwiches to my seat companion. This immediately put us on a footing of intimacy. From then on he became more and more confiding, buying me sandwiches in turn, which I could not possibly eat, what with the box of lunch I already had. Then when he told me to save them for next day, I foolishly mentioned it was Friday, whereupon I had long sermons and quotations from the Scriptures on man not being saved by meat or drink. At the next stop he bought me a fish sandwich.

As the night wore on my companion was begging me to share a drink with him, always in the most respectful, polite manner, of course. Finally my nerves became so on edge with his persistence that I had to leave the bus and wait over for another. Every seat was taken in the bus we were on, so it was impossible to change seats.

〇

Incidents like this, however, are rare. Usually you are in the company of workers, men and women, and they tell you of their jobs, or lack of jobs, their travels, their strivings, and sometimes of their religion.

There was another companion in Texas, a young Bohemian girl, a stenographer in Houston, who had been brought up on the land and was heartbroken to be away from it. Among the travelers there are often truck drivers whose cars have broken down, and they like to stand by the driver and talk of the hazards of the road. Just yesterday, when I was coming down from the farm at New-burgh in a blizzard, the driver of a milk truck came back into the city with me. He had taken his truck as far as Highland Mills and then had to abandon it to be picked up later. All the way down he saw other drivers wrestling with their huge vans and trailers and kept commenting on the struggle. "Mine was an empty, I couldn't do a thing. Now when I get to the city they won't believe me, how bad it is up here. The city's warm and melts the snow." You could feel that it was on his mind that he had not finished his job. He was bothered and resentful at the same time. He was old for a driver and looked worn and battered. His hands were red and chapped and dirty, and he clasped a red Manila folder—his papers, his reports, his job. You felt how much more important than he the job was, the way men have made things today.

Another driver who sat beside me on one of my cross-country trips was a driver of cars from Detroit. He had taken the bus back to get another pair of cars. He described to me how the efficiency "engineers" worked, estimating to the drop the amount of gasoline needed. One time he got behind a parade and the starting and stopping used more gasoline than the ex-perts had estimated so he had a hard time making it to the next stop. Not much chance to pad expense accounts on such jobs. The assumption is that all men are dishonest, and estimates are made accordingly. He explained how the company connived with the driver to get out of paying the special tax in some states, and how they shared the gain.

❦

As I traveled across the country this time, I found the buses more crowded than they were a year ago and more people talking about lack of work. "They keep telling us there is no depression," one man grumbled, "but it looks like it's coming on again." The last depression is still in their bones.

Food differs as you go across the United States, though not much in price. In Arkansas and Oklahoma you can get karopecan pie, which is as sweet as Syrian pastry and just as regional. All through the West you should eat chile. It is the cheapest and best dish for a main meal. It isn't the pure Mexican chile, but it's hot enough, and it is the same everywhere, made with red beans and meat and lots of gravy and crackers. A few years ago it was fifteen cents; now it is a quarter. But it is still a full meal and better than anyone can get on a railroad diner.

Yes, we have eaten on diners, and we have traveled in other ways than in buses. When I was coming back from Seattle by the Northern Pacific, by railroad coach, the seating was most comfortable, with wonderful leg rests that made it possible really to sleep soundly all night. But the radio blared all day. No amount of pleading with the porter or conductor would make them turn it off. The Western Pacific with its double-decker sky-view effect was most interesting, but the seating was not so comfortable, and up in the "dome" the fumes of the diesel engine seeped in and the rounded glass was hard on the eyes.

Peter Maurin almost always traveled by buses. . . . He was never so happy as when he was setting forth on a trip to speak, to visit our houses of hospitality and farms. Once when we were both speaking at Notre Dame and were leaving the next morning to go in different directions, Professors Emmanuel Chapman and Robert Pollock accompanied us to the station. They had been enthusiastically arguing with Peter all night and were still going strong that morning. In his absorption in the talk Peter started to get on the wrong bus.

"Look out, Peter, that bus is going to Cincinnati," Pollack cried. Peter answered debonairly, "Oh, that's all right, I know someone there." He was what I would call a real traveler.

We Plead Guilty

14

"We were, frankly, hoping for jail. Perhaps jail, we thought, would put another compulsion on us, of being more truly poor."

The most important contribution to thought made by the Catholic Worker, John Cort once said, was our emphasis on voluntary poverty. Whenever I am invited to speak at schools around the country and talk about the problems of destitution in this rich country, and in the name of the Catholic Worker receive praise, I feel guilty. When our readers and listeners say that I make them feel guilty, I can only say I feel more guilty. We live in the midst of destitution in a rich country, and when we sit down to eat, we know that there is a line waiting at the door so long that the house could not hold them. When we pass men lying on the streets at night, and see men huddled around a fire built against the old theater building next door, and we go into our St. Joseph's house of hospitality, into a house where men are sleeping on the floor (because all the beds

Originally published in *Commonweal* 67 (December 27, 1957): 330–33.

are taken) and we go to our own warm and comfortable bed, once again we cannot help but feel guilty.

It is hard to comfort ourselves with the reflection that if we did not get rest and food we would not be able to do the work we do. We can reflect that some of the poverty we profess comes from lack of privacy, lack of time to ourselves. We can list instances of sights and sounds, smells and feelings that one can never get used to nor fail to cringe from. Yet God has blessed us so abundantly, has provided for us so constantly over these twenty-five years that we are always in the paradoxical position of rejoicing and saying to ourselves "our lines are fallen in goodly places." "It is good, Lord, to be here." We feel overwhelmed with graces, and yet we know we fail to correspond to them. We fail far more than seven times daily, failing in our vocation of poverty especially. As we think of all this, our feeling of guilt persists.

For this reason, as well as for the reason that we are pacifists, we refused to take part in the war maneuvers, if you can call them that, of the compulsory civil defense drills of the past three years. We were, frankly, hoping for jail. Ammon Hennacy, one of our editors, frankly says he wants to be a martyr. And as for me, I feel of course that the servant is not above the master, that we must take up our cross and follow our Master. Perhaps jail, we thought, would put another compulsion on us, of being more truly poor. Then *we* would not be running a house of hospitality, *we* would not be dispensing food and clothing, *we* would not be ministering to the destitute, but would be truly one with them. We would be truly among the least of God's children, sharing with them their misery. Then we could truly say in the prayers at the foot of the altar, "poor banished, children of Eve, mourning and weeping in this valley of tears." How hard it is to say it, surrounded by material and spiritual benefits as we are!

And so on three occasions we have been imprisoned. Each time we have gone through the grueling experience of torturous rides in the police van, sitting for long hours in prison cells awaiting booking or trial. In the first year, we had only an overnight experience of jail (which necessitated, however, the examinations for drugs, the humiliations of being stripped and showered and deprived of clothing and belongings). The second year the sentence was five days, and this last summer it was thirty days (with five days off for good behavior).

When we were locked in that first night in a narrow cell meant for one but holding two cots, we had just passed through an experience which was as ugly and horrifying as any I may ever experience. I know that St. Paul said, "Let these things not so much as be mentioned among you," and it is not as a litterateur I speak, but as a Christian, who shares the guilt of all. We had been processed, we clutched our wrappers around us, and as we got off the elevators on the seventh floor to be assigned our cells, we were surrounded by a group of young women, colored and white, Puerto Rican and American, who first surveyed us boldly and then started making ribald comments. Deane Mowrer and I were older women though Deane was younger than I, and Judith Beck was young and beautiful. She was an actress which means that she carries herself consciously, alert to the gaze of others, responding to it. Her black hair hung down around her shoulders, her face was very pale, but she had managed to get some lipstick on before the officers took all her things away from her.

"Put her in my cell," one of the roughest of the Puerto Rican girls shouted, clutching at Judith. "Let me have her," another one called out. It was a real hubbub, ugly and distracting, coming as it did on top of hours of contact with prison officials, officers, nurses and so on.

I had a great sinking of the heart, a great sense of terror for Judith. Was this what jail meant? We had not expected this type of assault—and on the part of women. With the idea of protecting Judith, I *demanded,* and I used that term too for the only time during my imprisonment, that she be put in my cell or Deane's cell if we had to be doubled up because of crowding. "I will make complaints," I said very firmly, "if you do not do this."

The jeering and controversy continued, but the officer took us to our respective cells, putting Judith and me in one, and

Deane in another at the opposite corridor. Later, Joan Moses, a young Protestant demonstrator, who had gone alone with her husband to Times Square and made a public refusal to take shelter, and who was tried three days after we were, joined us, and she and Deane, and Judith and I, were put into adjoining cells.

ভ৹

We felt this sense of separation from the other prisoners, and as we were locked in that first night, I thought of a recent story by J. D. Salinger which I had read in the *New Yorker*, "Zooie." It is about the impact of the Prayer of Jesus, famous among pilgrims in Russia, on a young girl from an actor's family. The prayer is, "My Lord Jesus Christ, Son of the Living God, have mercy on me a sinner." Sometimes the prayer is shortened: "My Lord Jesus, have mercy on me a sinner." Sometimes it is accompanied by prostrations, sometimes by a way of breathing, "My Lord Jesus" being said as one inhales, and the rest of the prayer as one exhales. Eastern theologians warn against using this prayer without spiritual direction. Dr. Bulgakoff states that according to the theology of the Eastern Church, at the very mention of the Holy Name, there He is in the midst of us.

The girl Frannie in Salinger's story has become entangled in this prayer and is in such a state that her mother is about to get the advice of a psychiatrist. But the brother, who has been educated with his sister by an older brother who is something of a mystic, accomplishes her release from the hysteria into which she had plunged through a ceaseless repetition of the Jesus prayer, in a long conversation which makes the story more than a short story. He convinces her finally that she is trying to use a short cut to religious experience, that fundamentally she scorns others and is turning to God to escape from contact with humankind; and he reminds her of a piece of advice given her by an older brother. When she was acting in a radio play, as she had been the summer before, she was to remember the fat lady sitting on her porch rocking and listening to the radio. In other words, "Jesus Christ is the fat lady."

Part of the impact of the story is the contrast between the reverence (the Russians would have rejected "My Jesus, mercy!" as being too intimate) and, not only the last line, the punch line, but the irreverent language which leads up to it, the compulsive use of the Holy Name. The rest of its power lies in the profound Christian truth said over and over again by the saints, after our Lord Himself said it: He has left Himself in the midst of us, and what we can no longer do for Him we can do for them.

We were locked in our cells, and all the other five hundred women in the House of Detention were locked in theirs. The lights would go out at nine-thirty. The noise, the singing, the storytelling, the wildly vile language would go on until then. We were stunned by the impact of our reception, and the wild, manic spirits of all those young women about us. The week's work was finished, it was Friday night, and here were two days of leisure ahead.

I thought of this story of Salinger's and I found it hard to excuse myself for my own immediate harsh reaction. It is all very well to hate the sin and love the sinner in theory but it is hard to convey that idea in practice. By my peremptory rejection of the kind of welcome we received, I had of course protected Judith, but there was no expression of loving friendship in it towards the others. Lying there on my hard bed, I mourned to myself, "Jesus is the fat lady. Jesus is this unfortunate girl."

Jackie was released the next day; she had spent her six months, or her year or her two years, or whatever it was. One of the horrors of the House of Detention is that it is not just a place for the women awaiting trial as it was planned to be, but that it is used as a workhouse and penitentiary too, situated unsuitably though it is in the center of the city. A week later, we saw in the *Daily News,* which can be purchased by the inmates, that Jackie had attempted suicide and had been taken to Bellevue psychiatric prison ward. And a week after that she was back in the House of Detention, but on another floor.

ℰ◑

The other prisoners certainly did not harbor any hostility to us nor take offense at the openness of my judgment. It was my interior fear and harshness that I was judging in myself. We had not been issued clothing, and the officers were not going to allow us to go to the chapel in our wrappers. So our kind fellow-prisoners, sensing our keen disappointment, gathered together clothing, underwear, socks and shoes and dresses, so that we could go to Mass and receive Communion. Prostitutes, drug addicts, forgers and thieves had more loving kindness toward us than our jailers, who had no sense of the practice of religion being a necessity to us, but acted as though it were a privilege which they could withhold.

Of all the five hundred women in the Women's House of Detention only about fifteen got to Mass. By being importunate, I got to see the priest, to ask that my Bible, missal and breviary be permitted me. He was most reserved, withdrawn, and I had the impression that besides being aloof with women in general, he was most especially aloof with women prisoners. The chaplain was a man who might have been able to show a little warmth and human kindness and sympathy, but in addition to the jail, he also tended St. Vincent's Hospital and St. Joseph's Church. So we could not see much of him. On that day we obtained a small pamphlet Mass book and a diocesan paper to read.

Later, on the window sill in the dining room, I came across a copy of an old *New Yorker,* and in it a poem by W. H. Auden. He had come to my rescue the year before when I had been convicted of being a slum landlord. At that time he brought me the money to pay my $250 fine, a sentence which was afterwards suspended. It was like a visit from a friend to find this poem of Auden's. There was a refrain, "Thousands have lived without love, but none without water." This may not be exact—I am quoting from memory—but I know Judith sang it as she rejoiced in the one truly sensual enjoyment of the day, the shower. It was ninety-five degrees outside, and our cell was most oppressive. We indeed felt that we could not live without water.

Within a few days we were able to go to the library which is situated on the second floor of the House of Detention. It is a very good library and one can take out five books a week. Not that there is time to read five books, what with the work schedule each day. I borrowed *Resurrection,* by Tolstoy, that great story of a trek to Siberia of a concourse of prisoners, the royalties from which were donated by Tolstoy to pay for the emigration of the Doukhobors to Canada to escape the persecution they were undergoing in Russia for their pacifism. I had read the work before and had been especially impressed by the picture of the separation of the political prisoners and the ordinary criminals in the line. There was no such separation in our case.

I read *Northanger Abbey* by Jane Austen and was charmed by her defense of the novel form. I read *Embezzled Heaven* and travelled on pilgrimage with the old servant woman. *Kon Tiki* was a joy indeed and one could feel the spray of the open ocean on one's face and wonder at the great daring of these modern explorers. I was rather afraid to read Mann's *Doctor Faustus,* which my cell mate had taken out of the library—there was already enough emphasis on evil everywhere—but was happy to have my attention called to the beautiful descriptions of music which are in it.

The most startling thing I read in jail was a series of essays, entitled *Lenin,* by Trotsky, published back in 1926 or thereabouts. How had this book found its way into the library of one our city prisons? But I read it with interest. Trotsky described the moments he spent with Lenin when the revolution had become an accomplished fact, and Kerensky was driven out and Lenin and Trotsky had become the acknowledged leaders. "Lenin made the sign of the cross before his face," Trotsky wrote.

୧୨

But it was remembering Salinger, and Dostoevsky's Father Zossima, and Alyosha and the Honest Thief, and reading Tolstoy's short stories, that made me feel that again we had failed. We had the luxury of books—our horizons were widened though we were imprisoned. We could not certainly consider ourselves poor. Each day I read the prayers and the lessons from my daily missal and breviary to Judith, and when I told her stories of the fathers of the desert, she told me tales of the Hassidim. On the feast of St. Mary Magdalene I read:

> On my bed at night I sought him Whom my heart loves—
> I sought him but I did not find him.
>
> I will rise then and go about the city;
>   in the streets and crossings I will seek
> Him whom my heart loves.
> I sought him but I did not find him . . .
>
> Oh, that you were my brother,
>   nursed at my mother's breasts!
> If I met you out of doors, I would kiss you
>   and none would taunt me.
> I would lead you, bring you in
>   to the home of my mother. . . .
>
> Rejoice with me, all you who love the Lord, for
> I sought him and he appeared to me. And while I was
>   weeping at the tomb, I saw my Lord, Alleluia.

Yes, we fail in love, we make our judgments and we fail to see that we are all brothers, we all are seeking love, seeking God, seeking the beatific vision. All sin is a perversion, a turning from God and a turning to creatures.

If only our love had been stronger and truer, casting out fear, I would not have taken a stand, I would have seen Christ in Jackie. Suppose Judith had been her cell mate for the night and had been able to convey a little of the love the pacifists feel is the force which will overcome war. Perhaps, perhaps. . . . But this is the kind of analyzing and introspection and examination of conscience the narrator in *The Fall* indulged in after he heard that cry in the dark, that splash in the Seine and went his way without having helped his brother, only to hear a mocking laughter that followed him ever after.

Thank God for retroactive prayer! St. Paul said that he did not judge himself, nor must we. We can turn to our Lord Jesus Christ who has repaired already the greatest evil that ever happened or could ever happen, and trust that He will make up for our falls, for our neglects, for our failures in love.

Letter:
From Dorothy Day

15

To the editors: It was brought to my attention only the other day that Monsignor McCaffrey, chaplain to the women at the House of Detention in Greenwich Village, was very much hurt by my reference to him as not interested in the women under his care ["We Plead Guilty," Dec. 27, 1957]. I have written him a most belated letter of apology, but also explained, passing some of the blame on to you, that there were a few sentences deleted in my manuscript which changed the sense of that paragraph. If you will please print this letter, it may clear up his hurt, although I'm afraid it may hurt another priest!

I said that Monsignor McCaffrey had the care not only of the women but also of the St. Vincent's Hospital, besides his own parish, and that on that first Sunday morning, it was a young priest who offered Mass, who showed no interest in the women, but walked in looking neither to the right or left and that I had a hard time getting a few words to him, begging for a visit from Monsignor McCaffrey, the chaplain. The message was conveyed,

Originally published in *Commonweal* 68 (June 13, 1958): 282–83.

and Monsignor McCaffrey came to visit me, and was most kind, bringing me a Missal and magazines to read. I do not think that much more than a sentence was deleted from my original article, but it was enough to make it appear that it was Monsignor McCaffrey who was not interested in the women. When I finally got around to reading over the printed article, I was upset at the implication, but then it slipped my mind and I did nothing to rectify it. Now the matter has been brought to my attention, at this late date. I have written to the Monsignor to apologize and I would be grateful if you would also print this public apology.

As for the "young priest" I spoke of. It is a hard assignment, to come into a prison of five hundred women, and one needs special interest and the special grace to do the work. Not every priest is suited for it. It is not especially the age of the priest. I can see a young Father Hessler, the missioner, speaking with fervor, and loving kindness and warmth to the prisoners, telling them the lives of the saints, giving them some vision of a life other than their own, trying to awaken in them longings and desires for the love of God and for a life of grace. I am praying for such chaplains for women prisoners at the House of Detention.

Do print this letter soon. It will serve to remind your readers to pray for us all, and for all prisoners, all over the world. It is a forgotten work of mercy.

Pilgrimage to Mexico 16

I spent six months in Mexico back in 1929, most of the time in Mexico City and Xochimilco. The churches had just been re-opened and there was only one priest in all the capital who heard confessions in English. His understanding of the language was so bad he shouted to make you understand *him*, and the other penitents kept tactfully the church-length away during the long afternoon's wait to be heard. The political situation was bad, but when isn't it? It was a time of fiesta days, and every time the fireworks exploded we thought another revolution was starting. Diego Rivera was among the many Mexicans I met then. He was large and genial and had just come back from Russia, where, he told me, I had rubles waiting for me for the many translations into all the languages of the USSR of my article "Having a Baby," which had originally appeared in *The Masses*. It was a happy article and I was glad to hear that it had been translated. The baby, then going on four years old, was with me there. She had been baptized four

Originally published in *Commonweal* 69 (December 26, 1958): 336–38.

months after birth and I had been baptized eighteen months later.

I remember Rivera well, and I remember that I had been up against enough anti-Catholic and anti-religious propaganda among some of the artists and writers of *The Masses* not to be shocked at his attitude toward religion. I probably even agreed with much of Rivera's criticism, especially in regard to the wealth of the Church and the luxury of the clergy. But my Catholicism was an act of faith. "Though he may slay me, yet will I trust in Him." It had seemed like death, at the time, to become a Catholic.

The serious articles which I wrote while in Mexico about the political situation were all rejected by the Catholic magazines to which I submitted them. So I remembered the journalistic training I had received under Lionel Moise, the famed city editor who also taught journalism to Ernest Hemingway, and I began writing features about Tamar and myself. It was the beginning of Tamar's life in print and she has had to be content to be a part of my writing ever since. (Once when there was a long gap in my mention of her in articles a reader wrote to ask if she were dead!) I wrote about our visit to Our Lady of Guadalupe's shrine, about Easter in Xochimilco, about living with a Mexican family, about Adolpho Fuentes of the revolutionary party who took us on picnics in his truck on Sundays, about living with the people (Communists would call them the peasants) who farmed the man-made islands of Xochimilco.

I was there six months at that time and only returned to New York because Tamar became ill. And now I have spent another two weeks on a pilgrimage there. I presume to write about Mexico on the basis of just this much experience, but then Evelyn Waugh wrote an entire book about Mexico after only a two months' visit. He did not apologize, saying that it is the function of the journalist to "hope to notice things which the better experienced accept as commonplace and to convey to a distant public some idea of the aspect and feel of a place."

Ↄↄ

The two articles I wrote in *The Catholic Worker* about this pilgrimage called forth some sharp rebukes from critics of the Church who blame all the poverty and illiteracy of Mexico on the clergy. Who is their scapegoat for the poverty I have seen in America, that of the sharecroppers and the tenant farmers, the migrant workers, the Negroes and Puerto Ricans in our city slums? And why has not the revolution done more for the poor in Mexico in the hundred years since the reform laws were passed? But I do not want to enter into controversy. I will get on with my impressions, because that is all this article will be.

"But did you enjoy yourself?" Fritz Eichenberg asked me, after he had read my two articles in *The Catholic Worker,* and since they were apparently not personal enough for him, I shall make this very personal.

Yes, it was a happy trip. I enjoyed Father Neudecker's talk on the train between Kansas City and San Antonio and Laredo (and that part of the trip was most comfortable). I enjoyed the cartons of good whole wheat bread which he had baked himself at Kellogg, Minnesota, where he "earns his living" by grinding wheat and selling good flour as St. Paul earned his by sailmaking. I enjoyed his sitting up with us all night on the trip from the border to San Luis Potosi (accent on the last syllable), when it was freezing cold and the doors of the car would not stay closed. The old missionary with us took a berth, thank God, and the other priest, who should have, caught a very bad cold, but maybe it was Father Neudecker's whole wheat bread which saved him. The toilets overflowed, the car became filthy, but still it was not as bad as the front cars, which were of wood, with wooden seats and open windows.

Yes, I enjoyed that cold night—it was part of a pilgrimage. I enjoyed it as St. Francis did the ashes on his bread. Coming into San Luis Potosi four hours late, we received Communion at one of the three Masses offered, and then had our first solid meal at a little hotel. (Of course we had had plenty of Father Neudecker's bread.) Then our three guides drove us in their three cars over the most beautiful mountains and plains to Guanajuato, a town so entrancing that I should choose to stay there rather than at Taxco or Cuernavaca or any other tourist place. We put up for two nights at the Sante Fe hotel on the plaza. At night a band played and the boys and girls walked around and around, the boys going in one direction and the girls in another so that they were constantly repassing one another. When the band stopped, other musicians with stringed instruments and very solemn faces played Mexican music and sang mournfully.

℘

The next morning after an early Mass we set out for the Mountain of Christ the King, on the top of which is a great shrine, a tremendous statue like that of our Statue of Liberty, which was erected on this highest mountain of central Mexico to replace one which had been bombed by a lone Communist aviator back in 1928 or before. Perpetual adoration is offered at a shrine of the Benedictine nuns of Christ the King in a convent a little way down the mountain, which is seven thousand feet high. You can imagine the view of the world around us in that crystal clear air, high, high above the surrounding hills and plains.

One of the things about this old civilization is that no matter how far you go in the wilderness there are always signs of human habitation. There are no fences, but there are always shepherds and herdsmen, on foot, living with their animals, father and son, sitting with neighbor father and son. Oxen do the ploughing, harvesting is by hand, threshing is as it was in biblical times. The land is old, and the ways of the people are ancient, too. They are lean and spare and pruned to the bone.

The next day we started promptly at nine o'clock in the morning and drove in our three cars to San Miguel d'Allende, named not only for St. Michael but also for d'Allende, a national hero who (as one of the guides told us) pushed Father Hidalgo into revolution when he hesitated. We had an elaborate lunch there, in a hotel which was formerly a Franciscan monastery and is now the most luxurious building the town offers for travelers' accommodations, and visited the art school, which is also a former monastery. It is not only that the Orders were robbed of their possessions and of the fruit of their hard work; there is evidence too of a decline in vocations and the ability to build such foundations again.

We drove another hundred miles to Tolucca, and then on for forty-five miles to Mexico City. The city was a dazzling sight, a sea of jewels, as we came down the mountains into the old lake bed where the city is situated. Our hotel was spacious, with hot baths and high ceilings, but it was on a mean, narrow street. There was no restaurant in the hotel nor any near at hand, and the other pilgrims wanted to move, which we did the next day, although it was Sunday.

It is strange about pilgrimages. The high point should have been that Sunday morning, when we went out to the shrine of Our Lady of Guadalupe, three miles away from the center of the city. Street cars and buses, cabs, taxis, every kind of conveyance was directed toward that little hill of Tepayac, where the Blessed Mother, in the guise of a young Indian maiden of fifteen, appeared to Juan Diego (the Spanish name for the Indian) and told him that she would be the protectress of the Indians, that she loved them. Everyone knows the story, how she filled his tilma, a sort of burlap blanket he wore over his shoulders, with Castilian roses, which did not grow in that part of the country or at that time of year at all. He brought his roses to the Bishop, who, with those around him, at once fell on his knees in veneration. For there on the tilma was painted a miraculous picture of the Indian Aztec Virgin, Our Lady of Guadalupe. This all happened in 1531, and the best telling of it, from the original documents, is to be found in *The Dark Virgin* by Donald Demarest.

But the moment of exaltation does not come according to a timetable. We were on pilgrimage, and we had guides who had scheduled our tour—one day we were to be here, another there. Very often, of course, we did slip away from each other and kneel in those magnificent churches and basilicas among the people of Mexico City and among the poor, barefoot, white-clad, silent and devout, who kneel for hours, their arms outstretched, their eyes on the face of the Virgin or our Crucified Lord. It was all so different from everything we knew, that we had been accustomed to. We were distracted constantly by the crowds, and by the individuals who absorbed our attention. And there was the climate, the rarefied air at that tremendous altitude, twelve thousand feet.

಄

A pilgrimage like this is the time to be carried along with the others, to keep a diary, or to write letters home that will be saved for you to refresh your memory with. Later on, it is often a sudden smell of charcoal or beeswax, or the feel of cold stone under your knees, or the sight of another at worship that recalls you.

I visited the shrine again before we left, but I am always terribly distracted by people. No matter how long I stay, no matter how resolutely I try to close my eyes, ears and thought, my worship remains an act of will, a gesture of the body. I am present, but I am not carried away. Certainly I am more often overtaken by joy and thanksgiving in my own parish church at home. No matter how much of a pilgrim I consider myself, and call myself, I am wedded to home, to the house of hospitality, to the parish where we live in New York. It is my vocation.

On our last day we had an audience with Archbishop Miranda, and he kept us for two hours, talking to us about the Church in Mexico. We felt blessed indeed. The laws against the Church are still on the books, as they are in France, he pointed out. It is not only in Russia that the Church is being persecuted. The great need, he said, is for vocations, and for lay apostles to help the priests. This great archbishop is also a believer in nonviolent resistance to oppression. During the worst of the persecution there was not a bishop in Mexico who advocated armed resistance. Always the emphasis was on the spiritual weapons, on prayer and suffering. There were many martyrs.

Sunday, after Mass, I left on the noon bus, the Chuihuahua line, for El Paso, the ticket costing eleven dollars and fifty cents. The other pilgrims were returning by train or plane. The roads were good, the seats conducive to relaxed comfort, we were warm though there was a severe cold spell through central Mexico and I was overjoyed to hear one of my fellow passengers reading aloud, from a copy of *The Catholic Worker* which I had given her. She was reading some of Peter Maurin's *Easy Essays* to the only other English-speaking passenger in the crowded bus. Not at all distracted by the hubbub around her, she read and laughed aloud, and constantly said, "But this is remarkable!"

Peter Maurin, Catholic Worker founder, had reached a few more people, and I was on my way home, back to work with the new strength one always gains from a pilgrimage.

Southern Pilgrimage   17

Coming up from New Orleans to Baton Rouge—home of the Legislature which has five times fired the school board and appointed a new one, none of which has been accepted by the people—the highway is an ugly one, plastered with billboards and service stations and motels. Later on you come to a long, shaded road, shaded with live oaks, Spanish moss, a bayou on one side with turtles and cranes and yellow flowers among the patches of green along the water. But the town of Kenner, where Father Jerome Drolet lives, is still amidst the billboards. You turn to the left of them, go down a little main street and there, one block to the right, are the school, convent, rectory and white frame church. There is a lovely flower garden around the rectory, with sweet peas climbing up the wire fence, roses in bloom, yellow calendulas, and many other flowers.

Father Drolet had his picture on the first page of the *New York Times* in December, for joining in protest with a Methodist minister who went out to preach the gospel to the creatures who made up a screaming mob to persecute the colored parents es-

Originally published in *Commonweal* 74 (March 31, 1961): 10–12.

corting their children to the two integrated schools in New Orleans. Father Drolet, who is the pastor of his church, is a tall, good-looking man with a deeply lined face, still young. I first met him in 1937 during the seamen's strike, when he went around the waterfront collecting aid for the striking seamen in the strike which led to the formation of the National Maritime Union. He visited them in prison and in hospitals. "Blessed is he who remembers the needy and the poor," and they certainly were poor and persecuted that winter of the big strike.

Originally from Illinois, Father Drolet came to Louisiana and went through the seminary and was ordained priest to preach the gospel to the poor. Knowing that the gospel cannot be preached to men with empty stomachs, he turned to the works of mercy. But pastors often complain of the zeal of young curates, and Father Drolet found himself in Houma, Louisiana, among the sugar cane workers and shrimp fishers and cannery workers. (The minimum wage there is still fifty-eight cents an hour, he says.) Then he started a house of hospitality in a store front, opened up an integrated ball park and playground for the children, took in the wayfarer, but soon this too came to an end.

Time after time, too numerous to count, Father Drolet has made his voice heard, and time after time he has been transferred. I often think what good bishops these young priests would make. Being transferred all over the diocese, they get to know it as few others can.

I can see Father Drolet, rising up from his breakfast table, after Mass, after reading the daily paper, and going along that ugly highway to the beautiful city of New Orleans and passing through those streets of such beautiful names—Elysian Fields, Gentilly, Justice, Piety, Plenty, Benefit, Agriculture, Pleasure, Humanity, Desire. I see him standing there beside that intrepid Methodist minister whose house and church have been defiled, whose wife and children have been threatened, whose phone rings with obscenity in the dead of the night. And I am proud of this Methodist minister and this Catholic priest.

The opposition to integration, led by Catholics, sad to say, filled the Civic auditorium. The White Citizens Council takes the place now of the Ku Klux Klan. "It reminds you of the early days of Nazism," Father Drolet said. "They have a well-organized public relations department which provides material for press and radio. And people are afraid, afraid for their jobs. The press reported that it was the parents of the children going to the two schools where they were beginning token integration who were making the protest, making up the mob, but one should not believe them! They were not young parents but a group of much older women from other parts of town, manipulated to make a mob. Everyone is afraid and the police do not stop them."

"There is fear of course of physical violence," Father Drolet went on, "but mostly it is fear of losing jobs. And those people up North who read about these things should look to themselves too," he said, smiling. "We read down here about New Rochelle and Levittown, and Chicago, the housing projects, the discrimination practiced there in housing, jobs and schools."

Had he suffered from telephone calls and violence, we asked Father Drolet. No, but the White Citizens Council circulated leaflets outside of his church after every Mass on Sunday, stating that he was being investigated by the House Un-American Activities Committee. He and his custodian and his parishioners had tried to collect the leaflets from the windshields of the cars around. The custodian had been arrested. That's the heartbreaking thing about it, that it is the Negroes who are made to suffer, just as in South Africa when the priests and ministers open the churches to them and beg them to come in.

I was told by another priest who had seen the leaflet that Father Drolet was accused of circulating the *Daily Worker* when he was in the seminary. It was *The Catholic Worker* they were referring to, perhaps.

∞

Here in Baton Rouge I am staying in a colored parish, with members of Caritas, which is a new secular institute in formation, made up of Negroes and whites. We had been with the Caritas branch in New Orleans and had seen some bad slums—unpaved streets, sewerless neighborhoods, and sinking houses in the inadequately filled-in land of the town dump and the swamps. Now we were in the outskirts of Baton Rouge, in a more picturesque section, where the church, St. Paul's, is just around a bend in the road, and is a rebuilt movie house. The parish hall is a rebuilt saloon and it is there I am going to speak this "evening," as they say, though it will be only two p.m.

Father Osborne, the pastor here, has long been a friend, whom I first met at Collegeville, in Minnesota. When I arrived at the hall, there were some of his former parishioners from the little parish across the river where he had been for seven years. He has been only seven months in this parish but has already accomplished wonders.

Father Osborne is a large man of great dignity, especially in his magnificent vestments, hand-woven of raw silk, made in Switzerland and in Prinknash Abbey in Gloucester, England. Over the altar of his church there is a great crucifix, painted by Dom Gregory de Witte, a Swiss artist, who painted the colorful refectory at St. Joseph's Abbey at Covington, Louisiana. There are paintings of St. Paul on one side and Our Lady on the other.

There was a baptism here this morning before the six-thirty Mass, and the tall, young colored man wore a white garment rather like a chasuble, but simpler since it was two pieces of white linen cloth, hanging down front and back and joined at the shoulders by tapes tied. There have been seventy-four baptisms these last seven months. Converts have come from Southern University (colored), as well as from the neighborhood.

One might say that Father Osborne's parish is the first integrated parish under a Negro pastor. Perhaps his white parishioners from his former parish, where the white priest Father James Clement was his former pastor, led the way. The parish covers three little towns, Rosedale, Marin Gouin ("big mosquito") and Grosse Tete ("big head").

One of the teachers at the Shady Grove High School here was staying at Caritas with us this weekend, and she told me about a small group of the teachers at her school. When the trouble started, they recognized the danger of violence and loss of job, but they resolved on a course of action. They sent a telegram, also signed by twenty-five others, to the Legislature, which is made up mostly of northern and rural people who are against integration, and said firmly that they upheld the ruling of the Supreme Court.

Since then there have been community meetings discussing this, the latest a week ago. A town committee has been set up within the community to investigate the teachers, and smear tactics have been used. The additional twenty-five signers have been brainwashed, the committee says, but threats are made against them too. The community involved numbers only about two thousand people, which makes it all the more courageous for the thirty-one involved to take the stand they did.

Another outstanding figure in the struggle is Doug Manship, who owns the Baton Rouge broadcasting company and the television station. He reaches the public on the side of the few courageous ones with editorials which come out weekly.

One must not forget to mention Rudolph Lombard, student at Xavier University of New Orleans, which is run by the Sisters of the Blessed Sacrament. He was arrested in the sit-ins, and is now under sentence of sixty days and a two hundred and fifty dollar fine, which is being appealed. He is a member of CORE, the Congress of Racial Equality. He is a tall young Negro, a good student and well-liked by his companions. There are also the demonstrations of the thousands of Southern University students who marched on the State Capitol at Baton Rouge, and the eighteen who were arrested there.

ల

I felt when I left New Orleans that I had scarcely scratched the surface in finding out what was going on. Then, picking up the paper this morning, I read of fighting in Rwanda and Angola, in Laos and in Ecuador, where herdsmen and agricultural workers are battling the landowners with spears and war drums. Scattered and sporadic, these revolts are part of a world movement among the poor and despised.

Here in America, these educated students are using the weapons of nonviolence against discrimination, and we who are writing and reporting must tell of these things to give courage to other isolated groups who feel alone and ineffectual.

The National Catholic Conference for Interracial Justice concluded a two-day meeting in Washington, D.C., with this statement, referring to the 1960 Bishops' statement on personal responsibility. "There comes a time, and this is one in Louisiana, when private attitude and action is an insufficient display of just attitudes and of a willingness to do right . . . give open support to constructive steps forward, otherwise the racist will lead; and if such is the case, the right thinking but silent man shares the responsibility for this evil."

Father Jerome Drolet has done this. Father Osborne has done this, and so have these teachers and students I have written about. They have risked physical violence and loss of job. I have met with these people and without doubt there are more we don't read about in the press.

"Perhaps," said Father Drolet, the "South will lead yet, in this struggle, in spite of everything."

Certainly, and best of all, it is the Negroes who have furnished the inspired leadership of the countless thousands in the Montgomery bus strike and in the sit-in strikes which are still going on all over the South. The imprisonments of so many, the buffetings, the being spat upon, burned with cigarette butts, the ordeal of facing even with their little children the screaming hatred of mobs—all this gives so great a demonstration of nonviolence that it blinds us, perhaps, to the importance of what is going on. These are the weapons of the spirit, these sufferings.

'A. J.'   18

Death of a peacemaker

Abraham Johannes Muste of the War Resisters League, known to millions as A. J., died on February 11th at three o'clock in the afternoon at St. Luke's Hospital, in New York. He had not been ill a day. That morning he had woken up suffering pains in the back, and his doctor had urged him to go to St. Luke's. Soon after he entered the hospital he lapsed into unconsciousness and died most peacefully. His had been a long and a happy life of work for brotherhood and peace.

Muste had given us the story of his early life in an uncompleted autobiography which is included in a volume called *The Essays of A. J. Muste,* edited by Nat Hentoff and published by Bobbs-Merrill. He was born in a small Dutch town of so little importance that its name was treated with derision, as Bohunk is here. . . . His father was a coachman for a rich family who lived in what seemed to him a palace. His own family lived in one room, with alcoves for beds. He remembers having the job

Originally published in *Commonweal* 86 (March 24, 1967): 14–16.

of fetching the morning porridge from a community kitchen for the employer's big family, and how heavy the kettle was in the cold and dark of early morning. He was five or six then. . . .

When on the insistence of his mother's brothers, and with the offer of a loan for passage in steerage, the whole family spent two weeks at sea in midwinter with their own provisions, and the mother became ill and had to be hospitalized. . . . Because of her illness, they had to stay on Ellis Island for a month, and they used to play through the halls, with never a rebuke, because they were well-behaved children.

. . . One always thinks of the Calvinists as a dour people, but Muste's reminiscences are happy ones. At the first sound of the church bells on Sunday, a "jubilant" announcement, he calls it, the way to church and the time in church "are a delight, and the entrance into it, an entering into another world, the real world, the feeling which later I found conveyed in one of the New Testament Epistles, that one had come to the city of the living God."

He did not despise the "little way," the small incident. He tells of only one, and there must have been many, but he was not setting out to write a spiritual autobiography. The story he tells is of the mischievous boy he was, putting out his foot and tripping up a bully, older and larger than he, who had been called up for reprimand to the teacher's desk. The stumbling was taken as further horseplay and the boy was reprimanded twice over. The rest of the day the young A. J. knew that there would be an encounter when they got out of sight of the school, and he does not say that he was not afraid. When the meeting took place and the other boy's opening words were, "You tripped me," he looked his adversary in the eye and admitted it. Strangely enough, the larger boy turned on his heel and the anticipated retribution did not take place. Muste saw this incident as important; he had learned to face up to an adversary, look him in the eye, to admit the truth and not try to justify himself, and, most important of all, to overcome fear. I am sure that the "gentleness" that Père Régamey extols was present in his eye and speech, as it always was, and no hint of making judgment of a *person,* only of a way of acting.

That is one of the things I always felt about A. J., and one of
the reasons the young trusted him and listened to him. There was
little question of age difference. They were on the same side, and
they trusted him in spite of his age. There was no malice in him,
and so he found no malice in others. I am not saying that he did
not make moral judgments. His whole life was testimony to that.
On the one side was life, and on the other death, and he chose
life. He kept the commandments, and Jesus promised, to those
who loved God and their brother, "Do this and thou shalt live."

The first school A. J. went to back in Grand Rapids, Michigan,
was a religious school, and in first grade he was put to memo-
rizing the 119th Psalm (which happens to be my own favorite).
His sister started school when he was ready for second grade,
and from then on all the children of the Muste family went to
public schools. They could not afford the religious school run
by the Dutch Reformed Church. After all, his father had begun
his work in this country at six dollars for a sixty-hour week.

A. J. tells us little of his private life. He mentions that when he
graduated from the seminary in Holland, Michigan, he spent a
year in the ministry in a small town in Iowa, where he met the
young woman who was to be his wife. He fell in love at first sight,
married young and had a happy married life for the next forty-five
years. He got degrees from New Brunswick Theological Seminary
and from Union Theological Seminary in New York, and served
in New York churches, one of them on Second Avenue and Seventh Street. He became acquainted with the narrow streets of the
lower East Side, with the poor of every nationality clustered there.

He gave up his first fulltime assignment to a church in the
suburbs of Boston when the United States entered the First World
War, began working in Providence with Quakers, and was accepted by them in their ministry some time later. . . .

The Textile Strikes

Loving Emerson as he did, and following in Thoreau's footsteps
in his espousal of civil disobedience (he called it "holy disobe-

dience"), he enjoyed living in New England. Together with a number of other clergymen he participated in 1919 in the second big Lawrence, Massachusetts, textile strike, and took a leading part. It was only the first of many labor situations he became involved in, an involvement so deep that it took him for a time into the Trotskyist movement and led to a visit with Trotsky in Norway, at the invitation of that exponent of perpetual revolution. As secretary of the Amalgamated Textile Workers of America, Muste participated and led many strikes in the textile field and gained a thorough knowledge of the labor movement.

Peter Maurin was the first one of our Catholic Worker family to meet A. J. He had heard of him in Union Square as a Trotskyite, and when A. J. became head of the Presbyterian Labor Temple on Second Avenue and Fourteenth Street, he sought him out there for discussion. . . . Peter had read us Berdyaev's *Christianity and Class War,* and it was Muste's essay, "Pacifism and Class War," which had first interested him in Muste. The essays, "Trade Unions and the Revolution" and "Return to Pacifism," written in 1935 and 1936, clearly show what attracted Peter to Muste's meetings. Reading Muste's essays, as I am doing now, I am refreshed and stimulated and happy indeed that there is this record left of the life of a great and good man whose influence will long be felt.

Years ago, when we were having a conference of peace leaders at the Catholic Worker Farm in Newburgh one winter, one quality in A. J. struck me forcibly, and that is that there was no aggression in his speech or demeanor. While the Catholics felt called upon to express themselves vehemently, one might almost say aggressively, A. J. kept a peaceful calm that could not help but permeate the rather hectic atmosphere. There was a quality of silence about him that everyone remarked at the meetings which were held after his death, and he was not impatient to be heard, or to get his word in. He enjoyed listening to others, one felt, and was not just waiting to have his say, to be heard. And he had plenty to say. He could sum things up succinctly enough at a small gathering, but when he was invited to speak at a

meeting he spoke at length, with no gesturing, no "eloquence."
You listened to what he had to say, not to how he said it.

   But the last time I "heard" him speak, I did not hear him
speak, because I was behind the platform set up at Union Square,
and the microphones carried his voice across the square even to
the opposition that was picketing on the other side. The two of
us were there, both of us speaking, to uphold the young men
who were about to burn their draft cards in order to dramatize
most seriously their opposition to the war in Vietnam, and to
conscription, which forced eighteen-year-olds into an army
which was committing such atrocities against women and children with their napalm and lazy dog bombs, a war in which
every condition for a just war was being violated. There was a
terrible threat of violence that day in the air, in the crowd before
us as well as in the pickets in the distance. And that there was
hostility in this crowd was shown by the man who had a fire
extinguisher under his coat and turned it on the draft-card burn-
ers. Cries rang out—"Why not acid instead of water?" The water
was sprayed over A. J. and me too, and it put out the flames of
the draft cards but he stood there calmly as the counter-demon-
strators shouted, "Burn yourselves, not your draft cards!" A. J.
had spoken about the death of Norman Morrison, the Quaker
who had immolated himself in front of the Pentagon not long
before, and of Alice Herz, the Jewish refugee who was the first
person in the United States to offer her life in a flaming protest
against what men of her adopted country were doing to each
other at the other end of the world. It was two or three days after
that noon rally in Union Square that Roger LaPorte set fire to
himself in front of the United Nations.

❧

I cannot close this little obituary without quoting a few lines
from a book I am reading now. *The Two-Edged Sword,* by Father
John L. McKenzie, SJ, written back in 1955, an interpretation of
the Old Testament. Father McKenzie writes, "We must not un-
derestimate the creative powers of the human genius. . . . What

makes the history of the human race differ from the history of the anthropoid ape is the rare but recurring emergence of men who can break out of the framework of their times and initiate a new departure." I could not help but think of A. J. Muste and how in a new era of violence, he has epitomized the concept of nonviolence, in correlating the material and the spiritual, in this secular age.

A Reminiscence at 75   19

Dorothy Day, cofounder of the Catholic Worker Movement, wrote her first article for Commonweal *in September of 1929. To mark her 75th birthday, the editors recently asked her for an article of reminiscence and recollection. Her response follows.*

Dear friends,

I hope you do not mind my responding to your request for a short "reminiscence" by writing you a rather disjointed letter. I am inspired today by a great sense of happiness and gratitude to God and to *Commonweal* too and a desire to share it. I wonder how many people realize the loneliness of the convert. I don't know whether I conveyed that in my book *The Long Loneliness*. I wrote in my book about giving up a lover. But it meant also giving up a whole society of friends and fellow workers. It was such a betrayal of them, they thought. One who had yearned to walk in the footsteps of a Mother Jones and an Emma Goldman seemingly had turned her back on the entire radical movement and sought shelter in that great, corrupt Holy Roman

Originally published in *Commonweal* 95 (August 10, 1973): 424–25.

Catholic Church, right hand of the Oppressor, the State, rich and heartless, a traitor to her beginnings, her Founder, etc.

Anatole France introduced me to the Desert Fathers in his book *Thais,* and even in that satire the beauty of the saints shone through. George Eliot introduced me to the mystics. Her Maggie Tulliver read the *Imitation,* so I read it too, regardless of the fact that George Eliot rejected formal religion. Did you know that Tolstoy has Pierre read the *Imitation* after his duel with his wife's lover? That Gandhi and Vinoba Bhave have read the *Imitation?* And Pope John? It still nourishes me. I'm tired of hearing eminent theologians disparagingly quote that line, "I never go out into the company of men without coming back less a man." But how much idle talk in all our lives, dishonesty, equivocation, and so forth sullying each precious day! I go down on my knees each night and say "Dear Father, Jesus told us you were Our Father, repair these slips, mistakes, even sins I have committed with my tongue during this day—the discouraging word, the biting criticism, etc." Even this article.

Of course "my bitterness was most bitter" over and over again, not at Holy Mother the Church but at the human element in it. But thank God, there were always the Saints. When I visited Cuba and recalled Fr. Las Casas and all he was reputed to have done for the Indians, a Communist friend said grimly, "Yes, but as a landowner which he originally was, he introduced African slavery because the Indians died under the hard work, and besides he liked them better than the Africans."

I looked at the biography of Las Casas in the *Catholic Encyclopedia* and found that there was quite a bit of truth in that.

God forgive us the sins of our youth! But as Zachariah sang out, "We have knowledge of salvation through *forgiveness of our sins.*" I don't think anyone recognizes the comfort of this text better than I do. I have not yet been attracted by the present tendency to bring everything out into the light of day by public and published confessions. Were we not taught by Holy Mother Church to respect the modesty of the confessional? Or is that a silly expression? But oh the joy of knowing that you can always go there and be forgiven seventy times seven times. (Even though you wonder, in your distrust of yourself, whether you *really* mean or have the strength to "amend your life.") I hope your readers can read between the lines from the above and recognize what my positions on birth control and abortion are.

When I visited Australia (where there is a CW paper, a house of hospitality and a farming commune of families) newspaper reporters on my arrival in Melbourne and Sydney asked me what was my position on the Berrigans, birth control and abortion. My answer was simplistic. I followed Pope Paul. As to the Berrigans, I did not know what the Pope's attitude was, but I was a follower of Gandhi and Vinoba Bhave and in spite of the Berrigans' innocently destructive tendencies, loved them both.

Thank God we have a Pope Paul who upholds *respect for life*, an ideal so lofty, so high, so important even when it seems he has the whole Catholic world against him. Peter Maurin always held before our eyes a vision of the new man, the new social order as being possible, by God's grace, here and now, and he so fully lived the life of voluntary poverty and manual labor and he spent so much time in silence, and an hour a day in church, besides daily Mass and Communion (while he was in the city), that all who knew him revered and loved him as the leader and inspirer of the Catholic Worker Movement. As for me, I am so much a woman, that I am the housekeeper of the CW Movement. And I am a journalist and well trained in that, what with a father and three brothers, all of whom were journalists.

To get down to my gratitude to *Commonweal* which helped to train me in my journalistic career. George Shuster, of *Commonweal* in 1932, sent Peter Maurin to me. Not only that, whenever the CW appealed for help the *Commonweal* staff (I could not name all that contributed to us), not only sent money and clothes. They even shared their yearly retreats which they used to make at Portsmouth Priory when they invited some of our crowd, editor or a Bowery resident.

Peter Maurin used to bring some of our brilliant young men, like John Cogley, to visit the editors of *Commonweal*. He told me that John should be an editor of *Commonweal* some day. Peter thought of the CW as a school always and when he started having nightly meetings those first years, *Commonweal* helped provide speakers, besides building up our prestige so that we got many famous men over the years. Space forbids listing them.

Peter was delighted when people praised him and even seemed to boast of the college presidents who listened to him. He thought prestige helped the work. "We need to build up the prestige of these young men," he said to me and he himself did it to such an extent that many a time he was foolhardy in his trust and estimate of others.

I must illustrate my own explanation of why I have accepted the awards that have been accorded to me in the past few years, by a little story. This is called "reminiscing" and serves to remind people that I am *very, very old*, as one of my grandchildren said to me once. She said it as she handed me a crude drawing of a ten-tiered, high-riser birthday cake, "because you are *very, very old*," she had printed underneath, and have nine grandchildren to eat that cake, she neglected to add.

The story is this. A girl called Katey Smith way back in '34 was sent us by St. Vincent's Hospital; she had been operated on for tumor of the brain. (She recovered.) She loved to join in all our activities and accompanied us on a picketing expedition one day on 34th Street in front of the Mexican Consulate because renewed persecution of the Church had broken out. A passerby asked her what the picket line was about and she answered, "None of your damn business."

I would feel like Katey Smith if I refused some of the honors offered me, honors which call attention to and pay tribute to Peter Maurin's ideas. I have refused honorary degrees because of my respect for Holy Wisdom, just as much as for my abhorrence of our military-industrial-agricultural-educational-complex-conglomerate. I compromised when I accepted the Laetare medal from Notre Dame this year. Fr. Hesburgh threatened to come to First Street and present it there if I did not come to the midwest. At the Notre Dame graduation and conferral of degrees, a dozen or so honorary ones, I could be lost in the crowd, I thought. So I accepted and could acknowledge my debts of gratitude to George Shuster, who is assistant to the president, and Julian Pleasants and Norrie Merdzinsky who with various Holy Cross Fathers and Brothers and students kept a house of hospitality going in South Bend for some years. The Pleasants, the Ryans, the Geisslers, the McKiernans and others kept the idea of communal rural living, and intellectual work and manual labor alive all these years; and William Storey, a professor at Notre Dame who has fed my spiritual life for many years by his set of books—*Days of the Lord,* excerpts from which gave me the energy this morning to sit down and write this very imperfect letter of thanks to my friends.

I write this from my place of semi-retirement at Tivoli, New York. The spirit of youth today rejects our old names, *Maryfarm* and *St. Joseph's House,* but still keeps the name "Catholic Worker Farm." It is not the kind of farming commune or agronomic university Peter Maurin envisaged, but we can boast that whereas the average age of most "communes" in the U.S. today, according to statistics (Stanley Vishnewski says), is nine months (if you know better, write to him), our own commune has lasted thirty-eight years. The first farm was started in 1934, and there are still old-timers here, John Filliger, Hans Tunnesen, Stanley Vishnewski, Marge Hughes, Slim, etc. The latter three arriving when they were seventeen. Fidelity, constancy, are beautiful words, but we must confess there is much plain stubbornness and very real poverty, even destitution, which holds us together too.

Thank you for your patience. If you don't want this letter-article, send it back and I will use or expand on it for my next "On Pilgrimage" column in the *CW*. Fr. Clarence Duffy who was with us during the war years used to do the like. If we cut paragraphs from one of his articles, he used to gather them together from the wastepaper basket and paste them into his next article.

Love and gratitude to all of you always.

Index